Globalization of Indian Broadcasting

Globalization of Indian Broadcasting

Sushil Kumar Sinha

Raj Publications

New Delhi - 110002 (INDIA)

Globalization of Indian Broadcasting

First Published in 2006

ISBN 81-86208-46-1

The responsibility for the facts or opinions expressed is entirely of the Author and not of the Publishers.

Published by : ***Poonam Goel***
Raj Publications
4855/24, Ansari Road,
Daryaganj, Delhi-110 002
Tel. : (O) 011- 30120939

Laser Typesetting : Aarati Computers,
Delhi-110 009

Printed at : Balaji Offset Printers,
Delhi

PRINTED IN INDIA

Preface

Today, television broadcasting is probably the most significant means of influencing the lives of people throughout the world. It is their information and entertainment super highway, besides a gateway to education. During the last decade it has made major advances. The traditional structure and role of broadcasting has changed dramatically. Besides unprecedented reach, competition and convergence of technologies, it has also empowered the consumers to choose their favourites. All these have been intensified by the more liberal Governments, of the 1980s and thereafter.

The entry of global media conglomerates has opened up a new visual world for Indian audiences. In true sense, it has brought the concept of "global village" alive. Different countries of the world who are geographically apart from each other are now connected with their TV screen world wide.

The idea of global television is about more than just news coverage and the enormous size of a mass, universal audience. It includes a technological component–represented by satellite and cable channels. It also encompasses a global programming menu of game show, sports, movies, sitcoms and soft news etc. Economically, it implies expansive vision of a capitalist dream i.e mass market, not only for global programming but global advertisements of products to global consumers having more negative effect than positive. All these had given rise to 'NWICO' as perceived by UNESCO in 1970s and 80s. This globalisation of television has compelled Doordarshan to follow its suits. The Government of India has taken vital decision in the past few years, for permitting to set up linking hub for satellite of linking by private television broadcasters from the Indian soil, amendment to the cable TV net–works (regulations) Act/Rules, introduction to Direct to Home (DTH) broadcasting, digitalization of transmission, and introduction of DD + (Direct) service etc.

If we move back in 50s, when Doordarshan, started in India it has modeled itself closely on Britain's BBC which was valued for its strong centralization and there by helped in consolidating the power of viceroy and colonial authority. The irony is that BBC from 1950s onwards, began to face commercial competition, but in South Asia, Governments maintained their monopolies on public service broadcasting till 1990s, despite growing pressure for autonomy from different sections.

Since 1992 Doordarshan has been obliged to seek 80% of its operating cost from advertising, placing it in direct competition with the proliferating satellite and cable channels. This has lead to a relentless pursuit of the middle class audience, the main target of the advertisers, westernization of content, narrowing of programme diversity and tendency to relay on commercial broadcasting to maximize its profits. Doordarshan in the initial phase of globalisation was mimicking satellite sector, dominated by few media players. But now in most cases it has developed its own programming.

In India where dual public-private system exists and the public broadcaster is still more watched, with approximately 8.5 crores television households then any other private competitor and is the third largest television market in the world only behind China and the USA, its healthy co-existence depends on Government policy towards Television. It will not be out of context to recall that virtually every country has developed its television broadcast system as a terrestrially based Government monopoly. Now it is high time to make it more competitive without loosing its national character. If this happens, it will certainly influence the evolution of global television patterns. Fundamentally, committed to the national audience with a more complex mandate and agenda and now increasingly competitive under the pressure of private operators, its healthy growth and co-existence depends on balanced approach adopted by the Government as well as broadcasters. In recent years Doordarshan has been shaping the market in a number of ways i.e; through promotion of domestic programming production and putting limits on foreign programming content, by capturing substantial income and grant in aids from the Government and utilizing it for further development of software and hardware, by focussing on multinational programming and by stopping the misuse of new technology which help in unrestricted growth of global television (through a proper regulatory system, i.e; TRAI). It is pertinent to note that on 02 December, 2005 Govt. of India brought a notification which state that any Govt. agency can now demand details of TV footage and the news channels have to comply with it, Ministry can conduct surprise check, Govt. agency can demand any kind of information from the channels, and channels found showing objectionable content can lose up-linking facilities. News channels also have to stick to the advertising code, the programme code and broadcast code as stipulated in the cable network Act 1994 and so on, so forth.

In short on the eve of an expected new global era for television it is domestic not international and regional broadcasting which is surprisingly powerful at least when measure in terms of programming. The change brought by the 1990s may have made foreign programming more homogeneous and technologically available than never before but the actual use of such programming in the schedules of most broadcasters continue to be quite small. Despite all this national public broadcaster remain a powerful force with large audiences and a strong interest on preserving not only their own roles but also an identifiable national television culture that justifies those roles. This realization of the size of the domestic versus international markets is of no small significance, linked together local broadcasters with its decent quality, locally produced alternatives are likely to find new and innovative roles to play, unforeseen by the proponents of television "global village". So it is the need of the hour that Public Service Broadcasting in India be made more independent -both of the market and of the Government to face competition from global television as it is here to stay and we have to move accordingly. In this context it is worth mentioning that recently Prime Minister Manmohan Singh has constituted a high profile ICT committee comprising several eminents and top-notch bureaucrats to examine the convergance of technology, role of information, communication and telecom in contemporary society and its evolution. This will certainly help in creating healthy atmosphere for the development of PSB as well as global television functioning in India.

The topic in this book includes Introduction, a brief description about the functioning of global television in India as well as Doordarshan, impact and spread of global television, globalization of advertisement in Indian context, programming content in respect of global television and epilogue.

Words are inadequate to express my gratitudes to the authors and editors, whose works and reports I have used in this book.

For the work of such magnitude, I owe my sincere gratitude to my colleagues working with Doordarshan and All India Radio, who provided me valuable informations and suggestions from time to time. I am thankful to my friends working in Delhi University and the Librarian of NCBC for using the library in connection with my work. I am also thankful to my family for extending full cooperation, without whose help I could not have completed this work in time.

Lastly I am thankful to Ms. Poonam Goel of Raj Publications for taking keen interest in the publication of the book.

25.3.2006 **Sushil Kumar Sinha**

Contents

1

Introduction

India presents a huge challenges to any broadcasting institutions that aspires to serve the whole nation. With existing social inequality such as caste, class and gender inequality found both in rural and urban India and with 70.0 percent of its population living in rural parts of the country, speaking different languages and regional diversity, the task to cater the needs and to fulfill the aspirations of these people is a stupendous task. Keeping in view the above factors in mind at the time of Independence in 1947, the concern with developmental issues made Radio and later television a national choice.

Before moving to Indian Broadcasting scenario let us look at the picture of Global Broadcasting which will help us to know that where we stand.

Television Broadcasting Timeline

After initial experimental television broadcasts

in different countries with different technologies, regular television broadcasting began in 1935. Private broadcasters were issued commercial TV licences in 1941. Some important milestones in TV broadcasting history are as under:-

- March 1935 - the German government began its national service. This was the first non-experimental public television service.
- November 11, 1936 - The first scheduled television broadcasts in the UK began.
- 1939: The first regularly scheduled television broadcasts in the USA began.
- 1941: The first sponsored television broadcast appeared in the USA.
- July 1, 1941 - The first commercial TV licenses were issued to WCBW (later WCBS-TV) and WNBT (later WNBC-TV), New York City, USA.
- September 15, 1959 - First telecast started in India in Delhi by Doordarshan.
- 1982: Doordarshan introduced colour TV in India coinciding with Asian Games.
- In between 1982 and 2005, Doordarshan has seen many changes, the recent being the Free to Air Service, i.e., DTH in form of DD+(Direct) started on 16.12.2004.

Indian television broadcasting industry consists of two major segments:-

(a) Doordarshan, the public service broadcaster, and (b) the private broadcaster which includes both domestic and foreign broadcasters. The mode of operation of these two segments are widely different. Unlike private operators, DD has a social responsibility and its operation and delivery of content is not related to profits alone. At present it comes under an autonomous body, namely 'the Prasar Bharati' (BCI) with effect from 23rd November, 1997. The main objective is to free the media from the government control so that citizens can exercise their fundamental rights to freedom of expression and to ensure that access to media is not privilege of the political party in power alone. Unlike private players, DD has a three tier programming service: National, Regional and Local. DD had to face many ups and downs during its 47 years of existance, till 90s when global TV establish its foothold in India.

Global Communication has made television "a window on the world". It has brought world events from the Olympics to the Gulf War into the household as they happens. It has also brought in programmes from other countries, for satellites do not respect frontiers; which also reminds us of M.Mcluhan (1964) 'global village'. There is a degree of globalisation occuring in the media. Countries miles apart now share common images through the buying of programmes from one television organisation by another. There development express the emergence of a New world information order - an international system of the production, distribution and consumption of information. A major feature of this development is the growth of global corporations (discussed in later chapter) which largely control what is available. Global media corporations are impinging to varying degrees- on national broadcasting regimes, through digital, satellite and cable systems.

If we look at the history of Indian television it has three phases leading to the evolution of its present status: the world's largest television network. (Doordarshan alongwith a large number of private cable and satellite channels).

These are as follows:

(a) Experimentation and Maturation (1959-1976)

Doordarshan started its telecasting in 1959 with a single studio in Delhi, which transmitted programmes for half an hour twice a week in the beginning. For several years, farm programmes for rural audiences, folk dance and music, and women-oriented programmes were the mainstay of Doordarshan programming. Development rhetoric in the early 1960s was strong in UN and UNESCO conferences and the role of television for rural development was studied in depth in the country. Chanda (1966) and other Committee Report also examined the development potential and profitability of radio and television in the country as it assumes tremendous importance in a developing country like India which has low literacy rate, varied culture and multiple language. In initial stage Doordarshan main function was to spread mass education which today has taken backseat with entertainment and information occupying the major chunk of DD's programme. Infact the first school television experiment any-where in the world took place in India in 1961. Similarly, the world first satellite instructional television experiment was also launched in India in 1975 with assistance of several partners and from UNESCO in particular, to educate people in rural areas on agriculture, health and sanitation and to provide supplementary lessons for primary school students. The launching of the ETV channel as a part of the SITE continuity project and later on launch of different educational channels to expedite mass literacy project, launched by the government helped Doordarshan in promoting its social responsibility.

Expansion and Commercialization (1976-1991)

There was no national network system until 1982, when Asiad Game started in New Delhi. Colour television was introduced, making coverage of the game biggest national and international events. The Asiad also shifted focus from educational programmes to sports and entertainment. Several other genres such as information based talk shows, quiz programmes, entertainment education programmes for children, film songs, and sports programme emerged in the mid 1980s, such as telenovela inspired "Humlog" consisting of 156 episodes ran for 17 months in 1984-85 and tripled Doordarshan's advertisement revenue (singhal and Rogers, 1988). Realizing the potential for serialised drama, various serials such as, 'Buniyad', 'The Ramayana' and 'The Mahabharata' emerged in the later half of the 1980s. The differentation of television programming in the mid-1980s is attributed to the increased commercial sponsorship for entertainment oriented programming and due to the factor of economic liberalisation and globalisation.

Liberalization and Globalization (1991)

It was an invasion by thousands of cable wallahs, Cable network had begun growing at the beginning of the 1980s. However, western TV popularity in India is traced to 1991, when CNN became prominent in the country for its live coverage of the Gulf war. The launch of the Star TV over India in 1991 and then especially the Indian Channel Zee TV in 1992, added to the impetus with entertainment programming. South India saw an opportunity in this and different TV channels came ups such as, Sun TV in Tamilnadu with Tamil language, Eenadu TV in Karnataka started broadcasting programmes in Telegu language, Asianet in Kerala started programme in Malayalam language besides hosts of other satellite channels in regional languages. This was apart from various Hindi channels, such as Sony, Aaj Tak, Jain TV, etc. to name a few.

According to Thomas (1996), there are about 28 satellite broadcasting services that are commonly focussed on reaching particular ethnic communities. Some of them have been mentioned above. These regional language channels also reduces the overall markets reached by the major broadcasters in different regions of the country. This expansion truely marked the beginning of the liberalisation and globalisation of Indian television.

The regular viewers of most of the foreign satellite channels programmes were a small minority who aspired for "western consumerism and materialism". These viewers were seemed to caught in the globalisation process as they vacillate between their own moorings and an imitated global life style. Certainly these viewers allowed themselves to be sucked into a global cultural homogenisation process: overexposure to high level of individualism, materialism and a self-centred world view. This resulted in visible repercussions on family life and ethos among them. But now most of these channels have adopted local culture, values and other social aspects to fit it in the global perspective; i.e.; Glocalisation of programmes have taken place on a

Table: 1.1 Content Distribution of programmes in Selected Seven Television

Broad Programme Content	Name of the Channel							
	Door-darshan 1	Door darshan 2	El TV	Home TV	Sony	Star Plus	Zee TV	Total
Contemporary, historical and mythological drama and serials	45	71	18	22	24	38	39	257
Movies and Film based programmes	10	11	46	6	22	12	10	117
Art, Culture, classical dances and music, religious discourse and region specific programs	13	10	1	4	2	13	12	55
News, political and current affairs	5	9	-	3	-	5	4	26
Education, social and environment	8	7	2	-	-	3	5	25
Uncategorised and other programmes	28	12	4	11	1	8	4	68
Total	**109**	**120**	**46**	**46**	**50**	**81**	**73**	**550**

* Frequency has been counted in terms of the number of programmes in each category regardless of duration, concluding all commercials and development of social messages.

large scale, attracting large number of viewers. All other channels have by and large tried to confirm to the 'Doordarshan Model' which position Hindi films & film based programmes at the top followed by serialised drama and other programmes. A glimpse of the content of seven Hindi channels (August-September' 1997) proves this fact. Content Analysis and distribution of time in respect of these seven channels are given in Table: 1.1.

Except for EL TV and Sony Television, all channels have news on weekdays. Doordarshan, Zee Television and Star Television telecast news seven days a week. While Doordarshan and Star Plus have news in Hindi and English languages, for the other channels the news is in 'Hinglish'. Analysis has shown minor stylistic and content variations in news coverage.

By and large, the political events of the country remain the major news story on all channels. Apart from commercials, the prime advertising spots in television are taken by public information services. These include development messages related to agriculture, health, education, and other government initiatives. Such messages can be seen most on Doordarshan and to some extent on Zee Television and Star Plus.

"Social marketing" through television has gained some respectability in the recent past and a number of television spots are being used to promote awareness of, for example, AIDS or child labour, Political debates and discussions on major issues of public concern such as population, pollution, politics, national integration, and other social and legal issues are also covered much more on Doordarshan. In contrast, the private channels carry fewer programmes related to the public sphere. (Table: 1.2)

Table: 1.2 Distribution of Time Devoted to public sphere per week in Selected Seven Television Channels*

Name of the Channel	Time Devoted to Public Sphere (in Minutes)	Time Devoted to Recreation and Entertainment (in Minutes)	Total Telecast Time (in minutes)
Doordarshan 1	1,564 (19.6)	6,416 (80.4)	7,980 (100.0)
* Doordarshan 2	1,185 (16.6)	5,955 (83.4)	7,140 (100.0)
EL TV	210 (2.1)	9,870 (97.9)	10,080 (100.0)
Home TV	510 (7.5)	5,916 (92.5)	6,426 (100.0)
Sony	0 (0.0)	10,080 (100.0)	10,080 (100.0)
Star Plus	1,005 (10.0)	9,075 (90.0)	10,080 (100.0)
Zee TV	945 (9.4)	9,135 (90.5)	10,080 (100.0)
Total	**5,419 (8.8)**	**56,447 (91.2)**	**61,666 (100.0)**

* While five channels telecast 24 hours of programming, Doordarshan 1 and 2 together telecast for 16 hours per day (Now 24 hours.)

* Now Doordarshan 2 has been restructured as 'DD News' with News and current affairs programmes.

satellite channels have vastly increased the volume of programming available and numerous niche channels carry specialized content to various target audiences not least young viewers. In developing countries, which has experienced rapid deregulation, many western style television channels now serve urban areas. Feature films, serials, drama, talk shows and music predominate.

Penetration of cable and satellite TV broadcastings in India has increased significantly. It has emerged as the third largest C&S television viewing nation in the world after China and the United States with approximately 41.0 million cable TV households at the end of 2002. (FICCI, KMPG, The Indian Entertainment Sector Report, 2003) The growth of TV channels and viewership has resulted in television achieving the highest reach amongst the primary media delivery channels as highlighted below.

Table: 1.3

(in Million)

Media reach%	Press	Television	C&S TV	Radio	Cinema
SEC A	78	88	70	24	12
SEC B	65	86	59	21	11
SEC C	50	83	50	20	11
SEC D	32	75	36	17	11
SEC E	16	61	24	15	11

Source: NRS-2002 (June 2001-July 2002).

The number of channels on air have increased to over 100 from only two in 1992. Among these channels mainly three channels, i.e., Star Plus, Zee TV and Sony TV are the main competitors of the National channel

Doordarshan. Several DD's channels are also available in the cable and satellite broadcasting mode. Satellite channels can be categorised under following segments:-

	Genre	Channels*
a)	General Hindi and Entertainment	Star Plus, Sony, Zee TV, Sahara Manoranjan, Sabe, Cartoon Network, Splash, Nickelodean, Jain TV, NEPC TV Home, BI TV
b)	Sports	ESPN, Star Sports, Set Max, DD Sports, Ten Sports
c)	News	Aaj Tak, NDTV 24x7, Zee News, Star News, Sahara Samaya, BBC, CNN, Headlines Today, NDTV India, DD News, Sun News, CNBC India, India Vision News, TVI, India TV, AL Zajira
d)	Hindi Movies	Zee Cinema, Set Max, Star Gold, ATN
e)	English Movies	HBO, Star Movies, ZMZ, AXN, Hallmark, TNT
f)	Music	ETC, B4U, Channel V, MTV, Zee Music
g)	Regional Channel	Gemini TV, DDs regional services, Alpha, Tara, ATN, Prabhat, ETV, Sun, Eenadu, Raj, Vijay, Uday, Asianet, Usha, Jaya, Raj digital Plus, Surya, Kairali, GEC,
h)	Information	Discovery, Animal Planet, Adventure One, National Geographic Channel
i)	Hinglish	Zoom, Star One
j)	Fashion	FTV, Trendz TV
k)	Business & Commerce	ABNi, Zee Business
l)	Children	Cartoon, Nickelodean, Pogo, Toon Disney, Hungama, Splash, Animax
m)	Religious	Sanskar, Aastha, Sadhna

* Launching of new TV channels and amalgamation of existing one with other channels, are taking place frequently. (as Sabe with Sony).

The expansion of satellite and cable networks has seen the spread of channels targeting specific ethinic or religious diasporas, such as Med TV for Kurds, Zee TV for Indians, and Space TV for Chinese, Vietnameses, Japanese and Koreans. Viewing is not solely passive and there are emerging multiple and complex ways in which these media are consumed.

Another major development has been in the field of programmes received from a large number of foreign satellites. There are two main types of programmes. (1) English language channels which are predominantly made for global especially the western societies, (2) Indian language channels which transmit programmes keeping in mind the Indian audiences and catering to different language groups. A typical subscriber receives about 35 channels at a time.

As mentioned above, the FICCI KPMG report also expect that due to penetration differential, the growth in TV and C&S households estimated to reach approximately 111.0 million and 64.0 million respectively by 2007. The C&S households are expected to register a compound annual growth rate of 9.3 percent over the period of 2002 and 2008 and reach a penetration of approximately 57.6 percent within TV households as shown below:

Table 1.4 Number and Penetration of Cable Homes in India **(in Million)**

Year	TV Households	Cable & Satellite Households
2002	82	41
2003	88	44
2004	93	49
2005	99	53
2006	104	57
2007	111	64

Source: FICCI KMPG Report.

Similarly, the extent of penetration of TV and C& S TV in the country can be seen in the table given below.

Table 1.5

TV Scenario in India

Base: Estimated Households (in lakhs)	Urban	Rural	Total
All India	566 (28.0)	1454 (72.0)	2020 (100.0)
TV HHS	424	432	856
Non-TV HHS	143 (28.8)	1022 (71.2)	1164 (100.0)
C&S HHS	273 (64.3)	153 (35.7)	426 (100.0)

Source: NRS-2003

According to TAM Media Research, C&S TV Magazine, May 2003 the top ten C&S channels are as follows:

Table 1.6

Market Reach of Cable & Satellite TV-top ten Channels in India

Channel Name	Type	Market Reach	Market Share (million Homes)
Set Max	Entertainment/Sport	8.3	12.2%
Star Plus	General	7.2	10.5%
Sony TV	General	7.1	10.4%
Zee TV	General	6.3	9.2%
Ten Sports	Sports	5.9	8.6%
Zee Cinema	Indian Films	5.7	8.3%
Star Sports	Sports	5.6	8.2%
DD2	General	5.4	7.9%
Aaj Tak	News & Current Affairs	5.1	7.5%
Star Gold	Hindi Movies	4.8	7.0%

Due to fastest growing segment in the television industry, i.e. cable and satellite channels, which was highly fragmented in the early 1990s, requirement for heavy investment and advent of value added services, such as Internet over cable, pay-per view etc. many small operators have entered in franchising agreements or have merged with large operators, known as MSOs. These MSOs are corporatised and have the financial ability to make necessary investment in infrastructure. In recent years, many broadcasters have integrated their business with MSOs in order to have greater access to the subscribers.

In 1985 there had been only 150 cable operators which increased to 12000 by 1992 and further to 1.0 lakh in 1995. This is a huge increase and similarly satellite channels also spread its influence, but the entry of foreign and private satellite channel didnot immediately impact the growth of Doordarshan on its market share. Meanwhile there was a rapid expansion of studio centres and transmitters in the post-liberalisation period to combat the spread of satellite channel. Diagram given below indicate this growth:-

The global development also shows distinct traces in Asia. Amongst others, the previously public service broadcaster TVNZ of New Zealand, has been fully privatized and has more or less been taken over by the American media market. Subsequently, TVNZ has cancelled its membership with the Asia-Pacific Broadcasting Union. Another example is the "Asian Business Channel" with its headquarter in Singapore. It is with heavy American investment, by no means, "Asian" anymore. Not to mention Murdock's Star-TV (Satellite Television Asia Region) with its daughter "Zee TV". (presently seperated) "Zee TV' is servicing the Indian subcontinent successfully in the local

Growth of Doordarshan Kendras

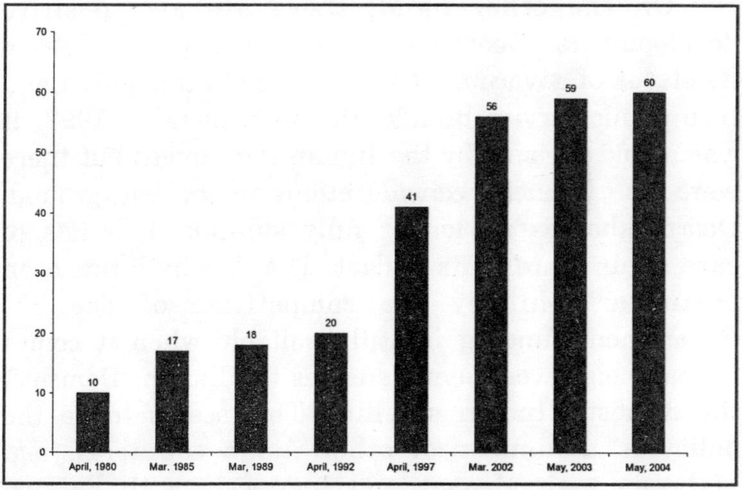

Source: Ministry of I & B, Annual Report, 2005

languages and has grabbed about 50% of the local market from Doordarshan. The deregulation and privatization now speeding up in Asia seem to favor such developments.

Growth of Doordarshan Transmitters

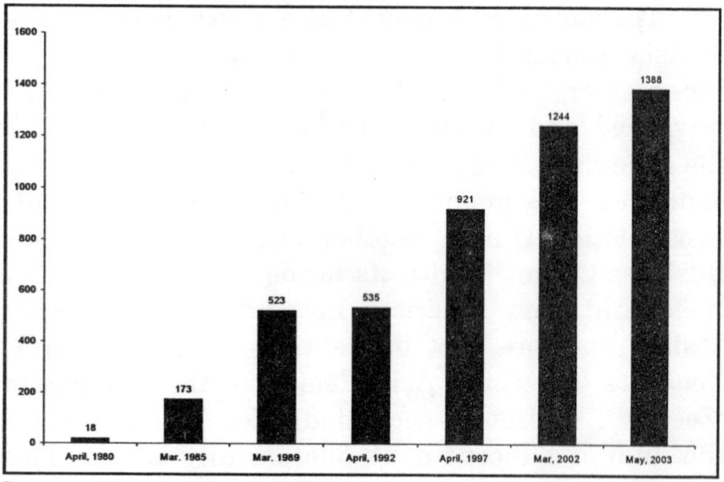

Source: Doordarshan, 2003

On the other hand, there are also positive developments. Doordarshan has been released from its status of government broadcaster to the status of a true public service broadcaster in September 1997. It was a bold decision by the Indian Parliament but there were also financial considerations in the background. Doordarshan is no longer fully subsidized, it has to earn a fair share of its budget. That is why it has been particularly hit by the competition of Zee TV. Government funding is still available when it comes to really big investments, such as the Indian "Domsat", the domestic Indian satellite. This seems to be the policy in a number of other Asian countries, e.g. Malaysia with Measat and Indonesia with Palapa. Another positive development seems to be on the way in Indonesia, there are initiatives to convert TVRI into a public service broadcaster. AIBD and FES are assisting TVRI and the Indonesian Parliament in this process.

But there is also an accelerated trend to reduce Public Service Broadcasting in favor of the establishment of private content providers and service providers. In Asia, lots of examples can be found. Some of these companies are listed below:

- Satelindo in Indonesia which operates the Palapa satellites.
- Astro with its home base in Malaysia which is the operator of the first digital direct-to-home satellite.
- Warf Cable in Hong Kong, thc owner of the first Video-on-demand network in Asia. Warf cable is already an example for content and service provider under one roof.
- Also Leo Kirch as one of the big European content providers is active in Asia since quite some time. The last Asian Games in Bangkok have been fully marketed by him. The official Thai broadcaster was just granted the terrestrial transmission rights in Thailand.

However the Indian-ness of Doordarshan is not an eternal essence but a contingent and contested social construction of a public culture in which the nation is ever more a spectacle- identified with consumption. DD is responding to the new competitors since 1990s with film programming and the opening up of the regional language channels, thus diversifying the range of Indian identities which could be based on the primacy of consumption. So there has been ideological shift in DD's culture from public-service to profit oriented programming. The growing commodification of information and the trend towards western-inspired entertainment can adversly affect the public service role of TV whose egalitarian potential remains largely under-explored in India.

Indian regulations relating to foreign investment in its television industry incorporate two principal policy objectives - (a) the need to maintain and encourage diversity of opinion, and (b) the preservation of Indian content in terms of editorial policy and control. The Indian's Government policy on television has been founded on the need to regulate all channels broadcast to an Indian audience, regardless of their ownership, origin or management and the ability to review, and if need be censor the content of foreign channels broadcast in India.

Television channels can be transmitted in India is one of three ways:

- Using a separate up-linking hub or teleport as requested by the proposed transmitter.
- Hiring an independent transponder on a satellite.
- Using a dedicated up-linking facility or earth station.

When the licence is guaranted to the party, it has to comply wth advertising and programming codes laid down from time to time by the I&B Ministry and has to follow the C&S rules and regulations framed by TRAI.

To regulate the unhindered growth of cable and satellite channels in India, way back in 1995, the industry was brought under a modicum of regulations. Overall the TV industry is governed by two main laws: (a) Applicable strictly to the public broadcaster, i.e, Doordarshan; and (b) regulation for cable operators and satellite channels. Doordarshan is governed by the Prasar Bharati Act, which was enacted in 1990 but came into force in 1997. Cable television networks are regulated by the Cable Television Networks (Regulation) Act, 1995. This act imposes registration and citizenship conditions for operation of cable television network. The other important regulation affecting operation of satellite channels through the cable network is the Cable Television Network (Regulation) Amendment Bill, 2000. This Bill states that all foreign and domestic satellite channels, distributed through the Cable network will have to abide by country's programme and advertising code. Prior to imposition of this Bill, only DD had to abide by the programme and advertising Code. The Bill has also imposed a "must carry" rule on cable operators, as it is mandatory for all cable operators to retransmit three DDs terrestrial channels on prime band, two national and one regional. The Cable Television Network (Regulation) Amendment Bill, 2002 makes it mandatory for the pay channel to be routed through a set-top box. The private broadcaster will have the flexibility to determine the rates for their pay channels. Another Bill, i.e., Communication Convergance Bill introduced on August 31, 2001 is lying before the government.

Although the 1995 Bill require the cable operators to register themselves but many of them under report the subscribers and charges any rate from them. As Bloomberg has estimated that 60,000 of these were not registered till the end of 2002, whereas 'The Hindu' put the figure at 26,000 (Narasimhan, 2002). So there arise the question of address-ability which can be introduced through the Conditional Access System (CAS). This system which is implemented globally, would increase transparency in the subscriber base and pay channels would get their rightful share of subscription revenue. The Cable TV Network (Regulation) Amendment Bill 2002 was passed in Lok Sabha and is now pending before Rajya Sabha. Also there are a number of hurdles in the process of implementation of the CAS. Successful implementation of CAS is likely to address the problem of under-declaration and hence result in higher share of subscription revenues for broadcasters.

In January 2003 the Govt. of India notified that CAS should be made effective in Chennai, Mumbai, Kolkata and Delhi by July 14, 2003. By a further notification in August, 2005, Delhi was excluded from the implementation of CAS, which was challenged by various writ petitions. Chennai was the only city that rolled out CAS on September 1, 2003 deadline. The Govt., by a further notification dated 27th February 2004 suspended the implementation of CAS until further notification. In this regard Madras High Court granted an interim stay on the implementation of the above notification. Without removing hurdles for implementation of CAS, transparency cannot be brought in the broadcasting industry.

Union Government also tried to regulate the contents, especially of news and current affairs channels by regulating the uplinking facilities to satellite channels. During the initial years of the growth of these channels, VSNL was the sole provider of uplinking facilities in India and most foreign satellite channels used to uplink from countries such as Hong Kong, Singapore and Thailand. Over the years, the government has significantly liberalised the uplinking policy and as per the new policy, an Indian private company which need not be a broadcaster, is permitted to set up uplinking hub/teleport facilities for purpose of hiring out/licencing to broadcaster. The new policy permit any television channel which is aimed at Indian Viewership irrespective of its ownership, equity structure or management control to uplink from India. In July 2000, the Ministry of I&B, Govt., of India issued guidelines in this context and it also facilitated Indian News agencies to have their own uplinking facilities for the purposes of news gathering and its further distribution to other news agencies or broadcaster. Further on March 26, 2003 the Govt. introduced guidelines for uplinking of news and current affairs TV channels from India, which were further amended on August 26, 2003, involved PIB besides Ministry of Home Affairs and other Ministries/ Departments concerned of the Government of India.

Besides the above mentioned regulations, most of the private and satellite channels, self-censored their programme contents and also follow certain content code, e.g. Star India follows the Star TV Hongkong code and currently certain other broadcasters follow the programming codes of the country they uplink from — mainly Hongkong and Singapore. Singapore has a Censorship Review Committee while Hongkong has a family viewing Policy which clearly specifies the hours meant for family viewing.

Despite all these regulatory mechanism, cable and satellite channels are broadcasting programmes which are not worth viewing, e.g. AXN programme 'Hot N wild', Star world-Temptation Island', Regional language channels especially in South, e.g; Sun TV, Gemini, etc.;

airing 'B' grade movie in late night show. There is no censorship applicable on Music videos-which today have the most objectionable and vulgar content. A lot of objections have been raised against the influx of raunchy music videos, especially the remixes such as 'Chadti Jawani', 'Kaanta Laga' etc. However, these videos are aired regularly throughout the day on all music channels including Southern Spice, MTV, ETC, Zee Music, ITV, Channel [V]. Though, recently, some music channel have started a system of internal checks. Similarly English movies channel e.g. HBO, Star Movies follow international codes and clearly specify the age group for whom the movies is suitable to view. The ASCI also check the content of advertisements to be aired on private and satellite channels. DD has its own code of conduct for advertisement. Inspite this surrogate advertisement is going on in advertisement of tobacco and liquor. The government could actually go ahead and set up its own regulatory bodies such as BRAI, and TRAI but again there should be check on the content of all channels at regular intervals and stringent punishment should be placed on violating the code of conducts. Again, the code and its norms should be dynamic, keeping in mind that our society is fast evolving. Keeping in view this fact, Ministry of I&B in collaboration with FICCI has drafted rules on self-regulation module which says that each programme has to be certified stating its timing and who can view it. The new set of rules and regulations are likely to come into force from mid-2006.

India has imposed some commercial presence restrictions in television broadcasting. For instance, private players are not allowed to enter the terrestrial broadcasting sector and foreign investment in DTH services is limited to a maximum of 49.0 percent. Since India has allowed foreign satellite channels to operate in the country, it can offer commitments in television transmission and broadcasting subject to the existing regulations.

Prior to 1985, the programmes telecast through Doordarshan were either produced in house or acquired from overseas. In 1985, Doordarshan started commissioning programmes to private production houses and this marked the beginning of Indian television programme producing companies. The mushrooming of satellite channels created a significant demand for local programming and this further boosted the development of the programming industry. From a few production houses catering to the public broadcaster, the software producing industry is now characterised by large corporations catering to both the domestic and international markets. From an importer of television content, India is becoming a hub for television software exports and Indian companies are trying to gain presence across varied media platforms. The electronic and computer software exports promotion council estimated that exports of television content was around US $ 74 million during 2001. (20.0% of total content revenue). After mid-1990s Indian companies started expanding into the global market, due to demand for Indian language programmes. Repatriate Indian maintain a close cultural and linguistic tie with their motherland and there is a growing demand for Indian language programmes from NRI. To meet this demand, many broadcasters such as Zee Telefilms Ltd., B4U Television Network India and Sony Entertainment Television have set up operations abroad. For instance, in 2001, Zee TV had more than 30 million viewers across 51 countries. Doordarshan too, have launched its international channel, DD-India in 1995. This channel currently reaches more than 50 countries in the world.

Invasion from Sky has to some extent tampered with the Indian cultural ethos and values, at least for some groups of viewers. So careful consideration is required to divert India from the path of social destruction arising from an on-going globalisation and homo-genisations of life styles.

In nutshell, some major achievements of Doordarshan and cables satellite TV has been presented below:

a) 1960s-1990s:- Government efforts at using TV for development communication have met with varying degrees of success. Major projects include SITE (75-76), Kheda Project (1976-1989), and the GRAMSAT experiment and Jhabua experiment.

b) 1981-1985: Rapid increase in the TV transmitters, one transmitter per day was the buzzword & introduction of colour TV.

c) 1984-85: launch of India's first major soap opera 'Humlog'. Increased telecast of film-based entertainment programmes, start of private sponsorship etc.

d) 1990: Prasar Bharati Act passed, delinking broadcasting from direct Govt. control. The Act was notified only in 1997.

e) 1991: Advent of Satellite channel; i.e.; CNN with Gulf war, later on other satellite channels also followed.

f) 1996-1997: Bill for regulations and guidelines for private and satellite TV channels working in India. Cost of TV advertising has increased by 329.0% between 1985 and 1997.

g) 2000 onward: Introduction of CAS, DD + direct, DTH services for TV viewers.

h) Number of programmes hours increased from 1500 per month to 25,000.

i) 50.8% of TV programmes content is entertainment followed by 13.3% of News and 9.6% of education and rest by others.

j) Doordarshan has a population reach of 330 million whereas satellite channels reach a population of 70 million.

k) 53.1% of DD's programmes are in Hindi, 21.2% in English and 25.7% in other languages. In case of satellite channels, 28.0% of their programmes are in Hindi, 40.6% in English and 31.4 % in regional languages.

References

- Chatterji, P.C., 1987, "Broadcasting in India", (Revised), Sage Publications, N. Delhi.
- Doordarshan Annual Report (DD India) 2003, Prasar Bharati (BCI), N. Delhi.
- Ministry of Information & Broadcasting, Annual Report, 2000-01 and 2002, Govt of India, N. Delhi.
- Report of the Review Committee on the working of Prasar Bharati, Ministry of I&B., Govt. of India, New Delhi.
- FICCI with Arthur Andersen India Pvt. Ltd. "Indian Entertainment Industry: Envisioning for Tomorrow, March 2001."
- FICCI with Arthur Anderson India Pvt. Ltd. "The Indian Entertainment Industry: Strategy and Vision, March 2000.
- Mckinsey quarterly " Media and Entertanment, Different Issues.
- The Economic Times, Entertainment: 2001-02.

- Pathania Geetika "Ambivalence in a Star-ry Eyed Land: Doordarshan and the Satellite TV challenge.
- Mitra. A, 1993, "Television and Popular Culture in India, Sage Publications, New Delhi.
- TV Today Network Report 2004.
- Ninan Sevanti, 1995, "Through the Magic Window: Television and Change in India", Sage Publications, New Delhi.
- Thussu, Daya Kishan "Taming the Dragon and the Elephant: Murdoch's Media in Asia.
- K. Rampal, "Cultural Bane or Sociological Boon? Impact of Satellite TV on Urban Youth in India. Feb-March-2003, Numero (RP).
- Bhatt, S.C., 1994, "Satellite Invasion of India", Gyan Publishing House, New Delhi.
- Bloomberg Television (2002)" Pay TV in the year 2002: Time for a Reality Check?"
- Telecom Regulatory Authority of India, New Delhi, Various Notifications.
- Joshi. Subhash, "25 years of Satellite Broadcasting in India," (Article).
- Thussu, D.K. 1998, "Indian Media-From Colonial to Global" (ed.) University, of North London.
- Thussu, D.K. 1998., "Localising the Global-Zee TV in India".
- Agrawal, Binod C. 1997, "The Meanings of Hinglishness: Liberalisation and Globalisation in Indian Broadcasting". Programming for People: From Cultural Rights to Cultural Responsibilities. Robins, Kevin, (Ed), United Nations World Television Forum, RAI, New York
- Hindustan Times, 19 February' 2006: "Real fun begins at night".

2

Doordarshan and Satellite Channels: A Profile

(A) State-owned TV Channels

Doordarshan occupies an unique place in the electronic media landscape of the country. As a national broadcaster, it is mandated to uphold the unity and integrity of the nation and to provide access to all the segments of the population. It has a huge infrastructure and offers a bouquet of channels with a wide variety of programmes offerings in Hindi as well as different regional languages. Thus in the present scenario, competing with different private and satellite channels. At present it is working under Prasar Bharati, an autonomous organisation, which came in effect from 15th September, 1997.

As a Public Service Broadcaster, it started its

services on 15th september 1959 with half an hour programme on education and development issues. A major landmark was the introduction of colour television in 1982 with Asian Game and from 1984 a phase of rapid expansion of Doordarshan took place with more or less installation of TV transmitter every day in the country.

DD-1: National Channel

It operates through a network of 1388 transmitter of varying power, covering 80.0% of the land area and 90.7% population of the country. It has three major component of Programme Content - information, education and entertainment. The information component consists of news and current affairs programmes. The education component is contributed by IGNOU, UGC, CIET, SIET and other sources.

In addition there are sponsored programmes like Turning Point, Adult education, National literacy Mission, Terra quiz and Bhoomi. Programmes on issues related to women and Janjatiya Darpan on tribal welfare is also telecast. The question hour in Parliament is telecast live on the National channel. For regional languages and dialects, there is a chunk between 3.00 pm and 8.00 pm. The entertainment programmes consists mainly of soap telecast between 12.00 noon to 3.00 pm and again between 9.00 pm to 11.00 pm, feature films telecast on Friday, Saturday and regional Award winning films on Sunday. The channel continue to make a significant and meaningful contribution to accelerate socio-economic change, promote national integration, create awareness and ecological balance and take measures for women welfare, children, less privileged etc.

DD-Bharati

Prasar Bharati launched this edutainment channel in the satellite mode on 26 January, 2002. This channel focuses primarily on music, dance, heritage, health, and children with special emphasis on the Indian way of life. It telecast programmes on Yoga and meditation, alternate system of medicine, aerobics and other aspects of health care in its daily health segment. It also feature programmes on cartoon, talent hunt shows, wildlife, news magazines by and for the children, campus scenes, counselling shows etc., for different sections of society. The programmes on the channel are a mix of in-house production, commissioned and sponsored programmes, live coverage of music festivals e.g.; Tansen Festival is done as an annual feature.

DD-News Channel

As a public broadcaster DD is providing balanced and unbiased news with out sensationalising as well as without carrying different shades. Considering, the perceived need for a dedicated news channel on DD's platform, the Prasar Bharati approved the proposal to start a 24-hours news channel in place of DD-Metro. This was subsequently approved by the Union Cabinet in its meeting held on 3 October, 2003 and consequently DD-News Channel was launched on 3 November, 2003 by converting DD-Metro into a 24-hours news channel. Its terrestrial reach is 21.6% by area and 44.9% by population of the country.

DD-News quickly gained popularity among viewers and for 2003-04, it earned Rs. 100 crores as commercial revenue. For the current year* (2004-05) it has already crossed Rs. 20 crores revenue.

---

* Ministry of I&B, Annual Report' 2005.

In addition to this round the clock telecast of Hindi/English News on DD-News, news bulletins in Hindi/English are also telecast twice a day on the National Network, i.e., DD-1. Regional News bulletin, apart from this, are also being telecast in various regional languages satellite service from 22 Doordarshan Kendras.

DD-India

This channel was launched on 14 March 1995. It is a complete India-centric channel giving an insight into the culture and tradition of India through classical, light, and film music, dance, films, news, current affairs programmes, plays and serials etc. This round the cloak channel is uplinked from Delhi. It reaches around 148 countries throughout the world. The following is the programme composition of DD-India.

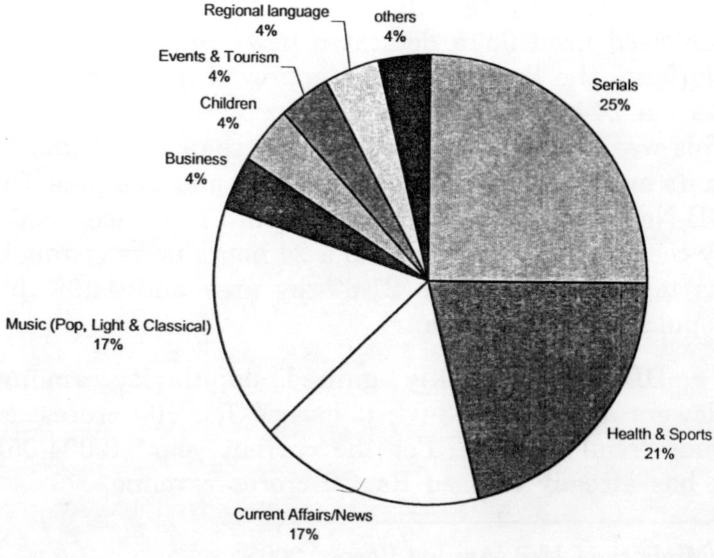

DD-Sports

Doordarshan made a history on 8 March, 1999 with the launch of DD-Sports Channel. From 1 June, 2000, the channel went on air round the clock. The channel was encrypted from 15 September, 2000 and once again it became free to air channel on 1 July, 2003. From 6 August, 2001, the channel is received in 34 countries in Middle East, CIS and neighbouring countries and European and African regions.

DD-Gyandarshan

The Ministry of Information and Broadcasting in collaboration with the Ministry of HRD and the IGNOU introduced on 26 January, 2000 a satellite channel-Gyandarshan-dedicated to education. On air round the clock, this channel beams programmes acquired from UGC, NCERT, CIET, SIERT and IGNOU. Gyandarshan on 26 January, 2004 went completely digital and expanded into a bouquet of channels, e.g.

GD-1: Best selection from other channels.

GD-2: Interactive Distance Education channel

GD-3: EKLAVYA-Technology channel

GD-4: VYAS-Higher Education channel.

Gyandarshan-2 is a one way video and two way audio satellite based interactive system operating on the C-Band of INSAT 3C. The Gyandarshan-III channel-Eklavya-dedicated to technical education was started on 26 January 2003 with different educational organisations.

Selected programmes of DD-Gyandarshan are also telecast on the National Network of DD-1 in the terrestrial mode. The content of programmes also provide entertainment along with information and education. To make educational programmes more attractive and commercially viable, DD has made collaborative arrangements with other Ministries and Government Departments for the production of such programmes in diverse fields.

Narrowcasting/Kisan Channel

Narrowcasting is the current buzzword in broadcasting. It involves the coverage of smaller areas with location specific programmes whereby the intimacy between the medium and the viewers gets stronger. DD has taken the initiative of introducing narrowcasting to address specific local issues related to the life style of the people residing in the coverage areas.

It started in 2000, initially involved 12 LPTs and included programmes of local genre telecast once/twice weekly. Study alone by the A.R. unit of Doordarshan revealed that the people of the coverage area has been benefited a lot through the programmes of Narrowcasting.

Based on this concept, a Kisan channel was launched in January, 2004, which broadcast its programmes five days a week, i.e, from Monday to Friday from 12 HPT's viz; Jalpaiguri (W.B.), Shillong (Meghalaya), Dibrugarh (Assam), Daltonganj (Jharkhand), Muzzafarpur (Bihar), Sambalpur (Orissa), Varanasi (U.P.), Vijaywada (A.P.), Gulbarga (Karnataka), Rajkot (Gujarat), Hisar (Haryana) and Indore (M.P.) Presently such programmes are broadcast for half an hour from 6.00 pm to 6.30 pm. The fund for this purpose are provided by Ministry of Agriculture. The service will be extended to other places in the coming years.

Some New Initiatives

In line with its constant endeavor to provide the best service to the citizens of India, Doordarshan took up many new initiatives during the year 2004-2005, and these are:

(A) **DTH Service of Doordarshan:** Free to air DTH service of Doordarshan (DD Direct+) has been launched on 16 December 2004, DTH bouquet presently comprises 33 TV channels (19 DD channels 14 Private Channels) besides 12 AIR channels. DTH signals are available in the entire country (except A&N island) and can be received with the help of a small size dish receiver unit. Multichannel service has become available in the entire country. 10,000 dish receiver unit has been provided for uncovered villages in some parts of the country. DTH bouquet for television is expected to be increased to 50 and that of Radio channels to 30. For Prasar Bharati, there are quite a few compelling reasons to go in for DTH. One of its main objectives is to ensure that DD and AIR programmes reach every household in the country, which at present is not reached by DD-1 or DD-2 (News services). It would also not like to be left behind domestic and overseas broadcasters in the race to make use of an advanced technology. Since the DTH system started by Doordarshan is free to air, the Conditional Access System (CAS) would not be required. This service is operational in the USA, Europe, Japan, Australia, Malaysia, Thailand, S.Korea, Taiwan, S. Africa and a few other countries. The competition in the satellite broadcast market is expected to intensify and in this situation DTH is going to play an important role by covering those areas which has not been tapped as yet. In fact, a far greater variety of choices would be needed to entice and retain subscribers in their region, i.e., of DTH.

(B) New studio centre at Gangtok (Sikkim) has been commissioned (60th) and the work on new studio centre at Dehradun is going on (will be commissioned on 15 August' 2007).

(C) **Projects in the North-East Region:** Five HPTs in this region have been upgraded from 1 kw to 10 kw HPTs and commissioned. Three Earth stations at shillong, Aizawal and Guwahati were completed and commissioned. Some special schemes (NE package, Phase II) have been considered by the EFC on 30 July, 2004, but yet to be approved.

(D) **Digitalisation:** Out of 27 DD's satellite channel, 24 have been digitalised and in the 10th plan, it will witness full digitalisation of 16 major DD kendras. 50.0% of the smaller DD Kendras will also be digitalised during this period.

(E) **Development Communication Division:** It has taken programmes in collaboration with some other Ministries/Departments of the Govt. of India, such as, Kalyani-1, and Kalyani-II, IRDA etc.

(F) **Uplinking Policy**: During the year 2003, the uplinking policy has been reviewed with regard to channels having News and Current Affairs contents; i.e.

i) The foreign investment has been restricted to 26.0% of the equity.

ii) all such existing channels should be brought under the new regime within a year.

These guidelines were revised fresh with regard to eligibility criteria from 28.8.2003.

27 companies have been permitted to set up 34 teleports in India: as many as 138 TV channels have been given permission to uplink from India through the permitted teleports. One News Agency has been given permission for News gathering and its distribution till date (i.e, upto 18.11.2004).

(B) Private and Satellite TV Channels

Despite the proliferation of cable and satellite channels the market is shared among three major players -Star, ZEE and Sony. Like media conglomerates elsewhere they have taken over similar competitions to present a mixed bouquet of programme offering to reach the diasporic as well as the national audience.

STAR TV: Star pioneered satellite TV in Asia and in the process catalysed explosive growth in the media industry across the region. In 1991, it started beaming five channel satellite service in English (STAR Plus, Prime Sports, Channel V, the BBC World and Star Movie). This became an instant hit with the English fluent urban elite. However, it soon realised that to make a profit the channel would have to make programmes in a language that a majority of Indians understood and on themes with which the masses would be able to identify.

Having been in the Indian market for over fourteen years, Star's fortunes in India changed dramatically after its flagship channel Star Plus launched "Kaun Banega Crorepati". The service helped

Star to become the most popular private channel in the country - with an average of 40 out of the top 50 shows every week. In 2004, Star claimed to be broadcasting its programme to more than 31.0 million homes in India. However, given the international nature of Star TV these programmes were reaching a large trans-Indian and even trans-Asian audience, as the Star bouquet shows:

(a) **Star Plus:** (entertainment channel).

(b) **Star News:** 24 hours news channel. It broadcast news both in English and Hindi.

(c) **Star Movies:** broadcast range from blockbusters and mainstream Hollywood output to all time classics.

(d) **Star World:** provides a complete mix of English language programming that is unmatched in Asia.

(e) **Star Gold:** Classic Hindi movies channel in India showcasing the golden moment in Hindi Cinema from 1940s to 1980s.

(f) **Star Sports:** It offers a diverse array of top flight Asian and International sporting events. Many of them lives.

(g) **Channel [V] India:** All music-channel available in middle-east, and south-east Asia.

(h) **National Geographic:** documentary channel

(i) **Adventure One:** Adrenaline-pumping action from around the world.

(j) **ESPN:** sports channel.

(k) **Star One:** Hindi entertainment channel.

While they started out with mainly western programmes, but later on forced first to Indianize, then regionalize and finally localize their programming to suit the range and variety of cultural and linguistic tastes encompassing the Indian market. It also popularised the use of Hinglish - mixing of English and Hindi language on its channels, for example "taste Kijiye Star Plus ka naya desi menu". Though most viewers choose Star for its entertainment programmes, there is also an increasing audience for its news output on Star News, which until April' 2003 broadcast news in both Hindi and English procured from NDTV, Star News was later revamped. In its new spruced up, youthful and flashier incarnation launched in the middle of operation Iraqi Freedom, the news network, now produced-in-house, and tended towards infotainment.

The I&B Ministry response to Star TV can be roughly classified under the following areas: (i) incipient cable regulation. (ii) privatization of programme content, (iii) changes in content and (iv) limiting access to uplink and foreign exchange.

Despite all these, liberalisation and globalisation of the Indian economy is the major factor behind Govt., toleration to the presence of this channel in India, besides strong presence of urban middle class.

Zee Network: Zee Network broadcasts 19 channels in the Indian subcontinent and several channels worldwide and reaches more than 250 million households across 120 countries. Zee TV, its flagship television channel that was launched in 1992 was the first Hindi general entertainment satellite channels in India. Its other TV channels includes:

(a) **Zee Cinema:** the first Hindi cinema channel in India.

(b) **Zee News:** the first 24 hours Hindi News channel in India.

(c) **Zee Music:** Music channel

(d) **Zee English:** Different mix of english programmes.

(e) **Zee MGM:** English Movies.

(f) **Trendz:** Fashion channel.

(g) **Alpha Marathi,** Alpha Bangla, Alpha Punjabi, Alpha Gujarati, etc. Regional languages channel.

(h) **Zee Sports:** A 24 hour encrypted channel which started on June 9, 2005, broadcast on PAS 10 satellite and is distributed as a part of the Zee Turner bouquet.

It recently commenced operating six new television channels, i.e. Action cinema, classic Cinema, Premiere Cinema, MX, Smile TV, and Jaagaran.

It is spread across all genres of entertainment and information through national, regional and english language segments. Zee is now uplinking 15 channels from India through a teleport of ASC Enterprises Limited.

Siticable Network, a wholly owned subsidiary of Zee is a multi system operator (MSO) with an estimated reach of 6.7 million homes in India. It has also started joint venture with Turner International India Ltd., for distribution of its 19 channels across the sub-continent alongwith 14 channels of Zee Network, CNN, Cartoon network, Pogo, CNBC and Reality TV.

Besides Zee Education, which focus on IT Education, it has began film production and distribution activities.

It was also the first network to elevate 'Hinglish' by using it in a more serious genre such as news, which had traditionally always been in either pure Hindi or in BBC English (Thussu, 1998).

After Star started making programmes in Hindi, it became a direct competitor for Zee, creating business rivalry between the two and in 1999 Zee brought back Star's 50.0 percent share in the company and also invested in the construction of 'Agrani', the regional satellite project for providing DTH Services.

Despite all these expansions of Zee network, less than 2.0 percent of its viewers live in rural areas (satellite & cable TV, 1999). Which donot fit with the concept of socially relevant television agenda pursued by different private TV channels in India.

Sony TV: Launched in October, 1995, Sony Entertainment Television (SET) is a Hindi general entertainment channel, focuses at providing quality and innovative entertainment to viewers across India. Over the year, the channel has created significant marquee properties through an impressive live up of programmes ranging from the light hearted to the supernatural, exploring various genres complimented by an explosive mix of glamorous events and Bollywood blockbusters. Known for its innovative concepts and exciting formats, SET has been providing strong platform for over 700 brands to reach over 35.0 million households in India.

SET is a part of the network of channels distributed by the One Alliance-a joint venture between SET India Pvt. Ltd. and Discovery Communications India. Other channels in this network include Max, Discovery, HBO, MTV, Animal Planet, AXN, ANIMAX, NDTV 24x7 and NICK.

The channel was the first to bring the Femina Miss India contest and the Annual Filmfare Awards to viewers. Besides this it telecast 'Asha Bhowsale' and 'Lata Mangeshkar's concert and was a big hit.

The serial 'Jassi Jaissi Koi nahin' an Indianised version of Latin American Soap called 'Betty La Fea' rescued SET from downfall and brought it back to limelight making it India's one of the most watched channel. In 2005, it created history with Indian Idol's, (On pattern of American Idol's) grand finale which rated to 14.29 TVR and was ranked number 3 on the chart. The next show in the pipeline is 'Fame Gurukul' based on the British format 'Fame Academy', and a second season of Indian Idol. It also acquired a commedy channel called SABe TV to target niche viewership.

Meanwhile Sony Music entertainment (India) Ltd. has entered into an agreement with Walt Disney Asia Pacific Ltd. to release Sony's entire catalogue of music records. Alongside, SPE, which holds 60.0 percent stake in SET, has set up a 100.0 percent subsidiary named Sony Pictures Films India to make and distribute films.

Besides the above, there are many other private channels. A brief description of some other cable and satellite channels (airing programmes in India) are given below:

CNN (Cable News Network): It was launched on June 1, 1980 and founded by Ted Turner. Currently it is owned by Time Warner. CNN is widely credited for introducing the concept of 24 hours news coverage. It has also launched many regional and foreign language network around the world. CNN global reputation was greatly enhanced in 1991 during the

Gulf war. Also on September 11, 2001, it was the first network to break news of the terrorist attacks on the United States.

Discovery Channel: It is an American cable TV network that has a variety of science programming particularly documentaries and nature shows. It went on air in 1984 and is owned by Discovery communications, which also owns TLC and Animal Planet.

Discovery channel also has a multiplex of digital channels: Discovery Times (operated in association with the New York Times), Discovery Health, Discovery Home & Leisure, Discovery Kids, Discovery Wings, Discovery Science, Discovery Travel and Adventure and Discovery Civilization.

Zoom: It was launched on 20th September, 2004. The channel is a premium, niche, non-fiction entertainment & life style channel in Hindi. Zoom intend to redefine entertainment viewing in India and increase its scope of entertainment beyond movies, music and Soaps.

As aspirations in India revolve around the lives of the Rich & Famous from fields like Bollywood, Sports, Music, Politics - the programming on Zoom has been created through celebrity-based shows. It is creating a platform where celebs and viewers can interface with each others. Its programme genres consists of : lifestyle & fashion, Music based shows, film entertainment, celebrity chat shows and game shows, Astrology and the paranormal etc.

There are 315.0 million Kids under 15 years in India which is one third of the country population. France with just 11.0 million Kids under 15s has 11 Kid's channels, United States has 24 with India having the least Kid's channels. Some of these have been mentioned here:

Disney Channel: It is a cable network run by the Walt Disney company in the United States, that went on air on April 18, 1977. It features family oriented programming, much of it aimed at pre-teens and younger adolescents. Most Disney channel programming does not feature the 'classic' Disney character such as 'Mickey Mouse', 'Donald Duck' and 'Goofy', but they are not completely absent either. The only actual spinoff of Disney channel is Toon Disney which features cartoons either created or distributed by Disney. Today's Disney channel includes two hit shows: 'That's so Raven' and 'Lizzie McGuire' alongwith shows like 'Phil of the Future' 'Boy Meets World', 'The Proud Family' 'Sister-Sister', 'The Famous Jeet Jackson', 'Kim Possible' etc.

Cartoon Network: By the end of the 1980s, Ted Turner's Cable TV conglomerate had acquired the MGM film library and in 1991 it purchased animation studio Hanna-Barbera Productions. The Cartoon Network was created out of the above two. In 1996, Time Warner purchased Turner Broadcasting and the cartoon network came under their corporate umbrella. Time Warner also changed the direction of Hanna-Barbera productions and focused the studio exclusively on creating new material for the Cartoon Network channel. Among the numerous shows the studio has produced are 'Dexter's laboratory' (1996), Johany Bravo (1997), Cow and chicken (1997), the Powerpuff Girls (1998), and the Ed, Edd,n Eddy (1998).

In recent years, Cartoon Network has also made attempts to attract viewers outside its core audience. Their mid-afternoon Cartoon Block 'Toonami' consists of reruns of acceptable for teens ainme from Japan, while a late night cartoon block called Adult Swin shows more rusque, teenage and Adult oriented Cartoons (e.g; Futurama and Family Guy). On April 17, 2004, Toonami was moved to Saturday evening and the afternoon slot was filled with Miguzi. In October 2004, Cartoon Network finally removed the looney Tunes show and additional classic cartoon programme makes to its schedule.

In September 2003, after just 11 months on air CNX was shut down and 'Toonami' became a 24 hour channel, in line with cartoon Network and Boomerang.

After Cartoon, Nickelodean and Splash entered in the Indian sky. Content wise both these channels have very little to offer, and most of the programmes broadcast are imported or at best dubbed in Hindi. Another three Kid's channels, namely, Pogo, Hungama and Sony's Animax is also broadcasting programmes in India.

Hungama TV: A UTV venture, marks the beginning of a new kid revolution: having apna point of view-by the kids and for the kids.

Some other TV channels operating in India

Aaj Tak : It was launched in 2003, followed by the launch of 'Headlines Today' in March, 2003 by the India Today groups and is a 24 hour news channel. At least 52.0 percent of India's urban population is watching it (As per NRS 2002), whereas 9.0 percent of young urban viewers watches Headlines Today (TAM November 15, 2003)

Aastha TV; **Sanskar and Sadhana TV:** All these

are socio-spiritual-cultural channel, now available 24 hours in India for viewers.

B4U TV: It is a complete Bollywood entertainment portal from the B4U worldwide network. It contains news, interviews, reviews, gossip and other trivia on Indian film Industry.

CNBC TV 18: This channel gives full information about the market, message board, mutual funds, insurance, debit and money, loans planning desk etc.

Gemini TV. It is a famous Telugu TV channel by Sun Network which is holding a bouquet of twelve top rated channels. Sun Network has got a reach, frequency and patronage than other groups.

India TV: Promoted by Rajat Sharma of Aap Ki Adalat fame. It is a news, views and current affairs channel.

India Vision, Kairali: Both are Malayalam TV channel providing and preserving traditional cultural heritage of Kerala alongwith entertainment.

MTV: MTV India network is a 24-hour music channel that caters to young Indians between the age of 15-34. However other age-groups also enjoy watching MTV programmes.

Maharishi Veda Vision: It offers scientifically validated knowledge of Veda and the Vedic literature as brought to the light by Maharishi Mahesh Yogi. It started broadcasting programme in India from 10th June, 1998 with the purpose of projecting heaven on Earth.

Sahara Manoranjan, Sahara Samaya: Started by the Sahara group, which has interest in other fields besides media. The first one provide general entertainment to the viewers, while the later one is a 24 hour news channel.

Trendz: Zee telefilm limited launched 'trendz' - A 24-hour premium fashion and style channel, on may 1, 2003. As a part of Turner bouquet, the channel is targeted at the fashion conscious Indian consumer. It provides in-depth analysis, new direction on the latest in fashion and style from around the world.

Raj TV Network: It was started in 1994 to provide wholesome entertainment for the entire family. With programme targeted at young and old, male and female alike the network has positioned itself as 'The People's channel.

NDTV: NDTV Ltd. was founded in 1988 and is India's first and largest private producer of news, current affairs and entertainment programmes.

National Geographic: This TV channel is a production arm of the National Geographic Society, the core supplier of the programme for this channel. This society entered into the partnership with News Corporation which gave birth of NGCI, formed in September, 1997. This channel is available through cables satellite on a 24 hour basis.

ETV: ETV is the largest network in India with 11 regional languages channels. It started with ETV Telegu in the year 1995 and is one of the most popular channel of South India.

ETC: ETC network owns two channels: ETC Hindi and ETC channel. Besides other items, it broadcasts general entertainment programmes.

Besides the above, there are programme production companies for different TV channels, such as, 'Nimbus Communication Pvt. Ltd., UTV Software Communication Ltd., Pritish Nandy Communication, etc.

References

- Annual Report 2004-05, Ministry of Information & Broadcasting, Govt of India., New Delhi.
- Doordarshan India 2003, Prasar Bharati, BCI, Directorate General Doordarshan., New Delhi.
- Satellite and Cable TV Magazine 1999.
- Nimbus Television Pvt. Ltd. Annual Report 2004.
- Indian Television Dot Com's Ad-wise 2002.
- Satellite & Cable TV Magazine, 2003.
- Thussu, D.K., "Taming the Dragon and the Elephant: Murdoch's Media in Asia.
- Broadcasting in India: Broadcasting Sector, July, 1999 Review.
- UTV Software Communication Ltd., Draft Red Herring Prospectus-2004.
- Indian television.com.
- Management Discussion and Analysis: Zee Telefilms Limited.
- Cartoon Network-Wikipedia, the free encyclopedia.
- TV Today Network Prospectus December 31, 2003
- The Tribune, July 1, 2005.

3

Spread and Impact of Global Television

The term 'globalization' was first coined in the 1980s but the concept stretches back centuries and beyond. The forces and events leading to globalization can be traced as far back as 1492 B.C., when people began to link disparate locations on the globe into extensive system of communication, migration and interconnections. In Indian context, it dates back to 325 B.C. Chandra Gupta Maurya was the first to triggered the globalization revolution by combining the expansive power of a world religion, trade, economy etc.; and imperial army for the first time connect India with many other parts of the world. From the day of Adam Smith till date, globalization has underwent sea-change.

Mediated Communication, especially the electronic

media like television has made the world a smaller place. It is not only that the electronic media has made messages more universally available but the diffusion of these messages has been potentiated in the last forty years by a series of sophisticated technologies. Television for example has become less a land based medium with limited geographical ranges around major cities and more a deterritorialized satellite based medium that can reach a third of the earth's surface with its signal. It has transformed global communication into a more common experience for most of the world's populations today.

Indeed television is the medium that has been most transformed by globalization but also the one that is most deeply implicated in facilitating globalization as a cultural process. Way back in 1964, McLuhan in his book **'Understanding Media'** had vision the unification of the world into a global village that emerged from the power of new media technologies such as, satellite, transoceanic cables and television networks to cross boundaries and increase international and inter-cultural communication.

But far from bringing about McLuhan dream of the 'global village', mass media is globalizing the world, constructing the new, shared worlds for the imagination of distinctive communities of sentiments and the invention of new scripts for their member's lives and for making public their concerns to both national and transnational audiences (A. Appadurai, 1996).

Infact the globalisation of television is often associated with the rise of satellite communication during the 1960s, which also led to the different communication theories and thought expressed by social scientists, as one mentioned above.

Another factor in success of global television is proliferation of installed bases of dish antenna over vast regions and progress in the miniaturization of TV technology on different fronts.

What these changes means for people's lives involve the third element identified by A. Appadurai, i.e., 'ideoscapes' : the flow of ideas and ideologies. On the whole, he has referred to global mediascapes as one of the five 'landscapes' of global cultural flow- the other being ethnoscapes, technoscapes, and finanscapes, - which have generated fundamental disjunctures between economy, culture and politics' in all societies over the last 20-30 years. Global broadcast media are globalizing in their form as well as their content and are controlled by corporate interests keen to expand their global market reach.

Some of the global media conglomerates operating in India are mentioned below:

Table : 3.1

Network or Outlet subscribers	Corporate entity World Wide	Households
a) BBC World Network	British Broadcasting Corp.	- 50.0 million
b) Cartoon Network	- Time Warner Bros.	- 140.5 million
c) CNN-International	- do -	- 181.9 million
d) Discovery channel	- Discovery Communication	- 125.9 million
e) ESPN	- Walt Disney Company & Hearst Corp.	- 250.0 million
f) MTV	- Viacom	- 310.0 million
g) NBC Network	- NBC	- 200.0 million
h) Sci-Fi Channel	- USA Network International	- 59.8 million
i) Sony	- Sony Corp.	--
j) Star Network	- Rupert Murdoch's News Corp.	--

The TNCs operate on multiple levels: global channels spread the same message in the same language, regional channels in local languages are established, with technical systems made available for this purpose. A few transnational media companies, most of which are based in the USA or Europe, dominate the spread of media products. Their cultural presence is considerably felt virtually on every continent. Lately, they have begun to establish themselves in the developing countries. Together with the World Wide Web, the expansion of media TNCs also has increased the paramountcy of English.

Table : 3.2: The largest media corporations in the world, by media sales volume 2001

(USD billions)

1. AOL Time Warner	38	USA
2. Viacom (Inc.)	23	USA
3. Vivendi Universal	19	France/USA
4. The Walt Disney Company	16	USA
5. Bertelsmann AG	15	Germany
6. News Corporation	13	Australia
7. Sony Corporation	9	Japan
8. Reed Elsevier	7	The Netherlands
9. Gannett Co., Inc.	6	USA
10. Pearson PLC	6	Great Britain

Source: Nordicom 2003.

Most of these companies are primarily involved in television and entertainment, but several also deal in news gathering and distribution. All control more than one medium and are thus been able to advertise and sell their products in one medium via one or more than one. Strategic alliances adopted by some of these media conglomerates can be seen from the table given below:

Table 3.3

Starategic behaviour of Western TNMCs in Asia

Company	Subsidiary	Strategic behaviour
AOL Time Warner	CNN International	- Strategic alliances with broadcasters (e.g. Doordarshan, India; YTN and MBN, Korea) and cable carriers (e.g. Cablevision, Singapore; Cable view services, Malaysia)
	HBO	- Joint veture with Sony to run HBO Asia
	Turner	- Joint venture with Zee Telefilms Ltd. in India (2001)
	Broadcasting	- Joint Venture with Tom.com to operate CETV in Hong Kong
BBC	BBC World	- Distribution agreements with Asian countries and regions like India, Taiwan (TV Time) and China
Disney	ESPN	- Joint venture with Star TV to run Star Sports
	Walt Disney Pictures	- Film distribution agreement with Modi Films International, India
GE	CNBC	- Joint venture with Dow Jones to operate CNBC Asia
Liberty Media	Discovery Channel	- Distribution agreement with International Broadcasting Corp. (cable distributor) in Thailand (1994)
News Corporation	Star TV	- Joint venture with two Hong Kong-based companies to operate the Phoenix Chinese Channel

		- Joint venture with Sony, Warner, Bertelsmann and Thorn EMI to develop its music channel, Channel V (1995)
Sony	Sony Pictures Entertainment	- Joint venture with a local firm in Korea to offer an animation-related cable channel (2001)
Viacom	MTV	- Licensing agreement with Star TV unit 1994 - Joint venture with Poly Gram to run MTV Asia (1995)
	Nickelodeon	- Distribution and co-production agreements in Philippines, Korea, India, and Pakistan (1998-2002)

The two important transnational corporations in the third world are to be found in Latin America. They are Globo in Brazil and Televisa in Mexico. Globo is the larger with a volume of roughly USD 3 billion (Variety, Aug 26-Sep 1, 2002). Having started out in the newspaper branch, the company now has expanded into television, pay-TV, music publishing and book publishing.

How these media corporates, spread worldwide is globalizing through their cultural products can be seen from the activities of 'Disney' and 'News Corporation'.

Disney

Disney corporation stands as an emblematic symbol of media globalization on the basis of near universal recognition of its children's film and television character most famously, 'Micky Mouse'. It has also marketed some successful media products such as animated films 'The little Mermaid', 'The lion King', 'Alladin', 'Beauty and the Beast', 101 Dalmatians and Pocahontas'. At the same time, Disney's control of the ESPN sports network acquired with the ABC take over has given it 'two horses to ride in the foreign markets, not just one' (Herman & McChensey, 1997).

News Corporation

News Corporation is perhaps the most truely global of major media corporations, with its phenomenal global reach, operating across different media. It has been most active in the Asia-Pacific. The Star network has also localised its programme formats for various Asian markets partly in recognition of the importance of cultural and linguistic difference to audience viewing patterns.

In the present scenario, these media conglomerates are spreading their activities in different cultural spheres including television and are also bringing global popular culture into the homes of audiences around the world. Indeed it was 'Sony Corporation', that brought home the reality of globalization in the USA. When it acquired columbia Tristar Film and television interests and CBS records in that country in 1989. Secondly, it examplifies a particular kind of global corporation, a media company that enters the media field from a base in industrial manufacturing.

While globalization of television has been going on since 1980s in India, demand from urban middle classes came around in 1991 for the likes of CNN coverage. Another media company, i.e., News corp., started Star TV in India, which was a major step toward globalization of television in India. Star with its five TV channels reaches to approximately 2.6 billion people in Asia. The easy penetration was due to:

(a) The existing broadcast based on an old system.

(b) The existing broadcast was State owned primarily a vehicle for news, education and social issues. Entertainment was usually films and film based programmes.

(c) While such things were useful for the rural poor, the growing urban middle class wanted more entertainments, soap operas etc.

(d) While television used to be rare in the past, they were now becoming widespread.

The owner intention was to reach at least the wealthiest 5.0 percent of this upper middle class who could afford to capture its open broadcast signals and it caused a stir throughout the region.

Similarly CNN with its 24 hours News service used satellite to beam its programme in different parts of the world and with reporting of the gulf war in 1990 it caused stir among not only U.S.A., but to global audiences. Many dates the globalization of television News from the time of that conflict.

As global media flows becomes part of the lexicon of urban India, more and more programmes and advertising depict a material culture which play on the aspirations of a large middle class who are caught in the globalization process as they swing between Indian tradition and internalizing a transnational identity more in keeping with global lifestyle.

If we look at the globalization of television, it all started with the sensing of USSR in 1960s about the development of Direct to Home (DTH) satellite technology and its ideological consequences for socialist countries which lead to no formal agreement among different member nations of U.N., but with the advent of Star after 20 years ignoring international legal practices the stage was setup for globalization of television. It can be argued that without STAR, Indian television might have remained a State monopoly with much less commercialization and for fewer programming channels.

The business of making and marketing television product was greatly influenced by the practice of global companies like STAR TV, AOL Time warner, Disney etc., Geetika Pathania has mentioned some business practices introduced by the global television companies, i.e., (a) Building of programmes and cable channels; (b) changing local taste in programming to suit global standard, (c) promoting global brands in advertising, and (d) adopting U.S. formats like 'Wheel of Fortune' or 'Who Wants to be a Millionaire' in Indian context.

Globalization of television has introduced the strategy of windoing 'or' reselling' a number of times a single film or television programmes for generation of maximum revenue. Again the large cultural linguistic groups will get programming aimed at them while those from smaller cultural and linguistic groups will not be served by global companies. These global television companies can invest large amounts of capital to make sure that their commercial and other interests succeed in the long run.

As mentioned, the power of global television conglomerates and the ubiquity of entertainment programming has globalized television impact and made it a logical target for accquisation of 'Cultural Imperialism' which can be narrowed down to 'Media Imperialism', ranging from the transfer of news, values, and journalistic training through advertising and consumption patterns to film and television entertainment (Boyd-Barrett,1977). 'Media Imperialism' occurs when one society media dominate another country's culture. The medium of television is a prime example to illustrate the effect of media imperialism. Similarly, cultural imperialism has been defined by Schiller in Communications and cultural Domination as "the sum of processes by which a society is brought into the modern worlds system and how its dominating stratum is attracted, pressured, forced and sometimes bribed into shaping social institutions to correspond to, or even promote the values and structures of the dominating centre of the system". What wallerstein describes as the world capitalist system is represented in the area of media by H. Schiller as 'global corporate cultural domination'.

Since television production largely depends on advertising revenue, it contents is determined by profits and does not necessarily promote national culture or national identity. The global corporations are seen as producing culture for consumption as commodities with profit rather than quality in mind.

Critics cites a 1999 anthropological study that linked the appearance of anorexia in Fiji to the popularity of American television programme notably 'Metrose Place' and 'Beverly Hills 90210'. Both series featured slender young actresses who, it was claimed, led Fijian Women (who are typically full figured) to question indigenous notions of the ideal body. Page and Crawley has also elaborated the form that media imperialism is taking place in the contemporary South Asian media environment. Hindi popular culture seems to be becoming South Asian popular culture. A Bangladeshi professional fears, "Hindi cable culture will become our culture. Another reports "In marriage ceremonies, traditional songs are disappearing and are being replaced by Hindi movie songs. In Nepal "the growing popularity of Hindi satellite channels is seen as undermining the role of Nepali as the national language". A Nepali discussant rues", the problem is our TV programmes try to copy Hindi programmes and these turn out bad". As far as Srilanka is concerned, the South Indian programmes are 'Indianizing' the Sri Lankan Tamil audiences, hegemonically impacting this community's reimaging of itself. The popularity of Hindi programmes in the word of one Pakistani media professional, demystifies the difference between India and Pakistan. Another finds that Indian programmes threaten Islamic culture even more dangerously than western programmes because the characters look like us, speak our language and have more or less the same culture and social values. Malayali channels reaches the diaspora in Srilanka, Malaysia and the Middle East with its programmes. Similar trends can be seen with Bengali channels with regional foot prints. Keeping in view the global perspective, even Doordarshan launched its DD-India on 14 March, 1995 which reaches around 148 countries throughout the world and is now a 24 hours channel. It is helping in building bridges with Indian communities living abroad and to show case the real India, its culture, values, traditions, modernity, diversity, unity, agony and its ecstasy for the entire world through high quality programmes that will inform, educate and entertain about Indian culture, customs and social life.

Many of these satellite channels in India are bilingual. Thussu, taking the case of Hinglish (Hindi + English) comments that its use has been the contributory factor in the expansion of Indian television outside the boarders of the country and he expresses his concern about an increasing emphasis on entertainment led Hinglish television which may be a cause of Cultural Hybridization in the globalized world resulting in linguistic and intellectual confusion. In this context, example of Zee TV can be cited. It popularised the use of Hinglish not just in youth oriented music programmes like 'Superhit Muqabala' but also in the News. Later on STAR and Sony also adopted similar approach to strengthen its feet in India. Another example in this series is of serial 'Micky Mouse and Donald Duck' on Disney channel. A. Dortman and A. Matterlart show this in their 1971 published book **'How to Read Donald Duck',** in which the Duck holiday trips turned into conquest in the course of time. The authors finding is that "Donald at home a wimp, uses his trips to primitive people - which undoubtedly represent less developed countries, in order to set himself up as their king". More or less Donald Duck activities have hidden ideology of the western countries.

In the initial stage, it leads to Hybridization of programmes, as for example Non-Resident Indians are spread all over the world. These people form global cultural market for news and entertainment and the transnational television has to cater to their needs through programmes. There are lot of examples in this context. As one of the Zee TV's earliest success was a popular Chinese serial dubbed into Hindi as 'Himgiri Ke Veer'. Doordarshan also screened a serial on the life of a young Japanese girl called 'Oshin'. This proved to be popular family entertainment and is a true example of cross-cultural hybridization, the impact was that many little girls have been named Oshin in India. MTV in India finds a hybrid Indian cousin in 'channel V', which demonstrates, media products that are destined to travel the world are likely to be culturally 'neutral' with a down grading of cultural specificity in themes and settings and a preference for formats and genres thought to be more universal. This also involves the 'deterritorialization of culture', for whom distribution takes place across the world.

Anxieties about the influence of global media on culture and values, as well as their direct political and economic power, were expressed at the international level through the New World Information and Communication Order (NWICO) debate. This debate which occured through the UNESCO from the early 1970s and was led by 'Third World', sought to use UNESCO and other international fora to call for a redistribution of global communications resources to redress international inequalities and enable the development of stronger national and regional communication systems in the developing world. It culminated in the submission of the MacBride Report **'Many voices, One World',** to the UNESCO in 1980, General Conference held in Belgrade but was declined in the face of hostility from the U.S. and Britain in particular, who withdrew their funding from UNESCO in 1985.

Cultural or Media Imperialism relies on the 'Hypodermic Model of Media effect', (Liebes & Katz, 1990) which assumes that the media content has a direct, unmediated impact on the audience behaviour. Cultural Imperialism therefore totally discounts an audiences' ability to actively interpret or dismiss media content rather than simply mirror and map the media's portroyal of accounts on their own, which is not true in the present scenario.

In the late 80s and early 90s, media scholars started to discredit the cultural imperialism hypothesis. These scholars argued that the theory failed to see the complexity of global flows, including the occurance of 'reverse colonization' nor it takes into account the 'localization' of cultural exports, the growth of national producers and international exporters in the third world and strong local resistance to cultural domination. In this context Gramci's notion of hegemony which uses dominant class interest on subaltern classes by state appratus has been argued by Martin-Barbero, who is of the view that popular culture has the power to transform and resist the dominant cultures through a complex process of mediation.

Secondly, different countries are censoring the programmes aired by global television which intend to or is polluting their culture and customs. For this Govt; of India has formulated uplinking policy for foreign satellite channels and also keep watch on the programme contents and TRAI has been entrusted the job which will be taken over by a new organisations if Bill pertaining to it (convergence Bill) is passed in the Parliament. As some satellite channels with western programming is serving as an instrument of ideological penetration and cultural pollution in South Asian context (Chadha & Kavoori, 2000). The Association of South East Asian Nations even went so far on issuing a statement expressing the need to formalise united response to the phenomenon of cultural globalization in order to protect and advance the cherised Asian Values and traditions that are being threatened by the proliferation of western media content (Herman & MCchesney, 1997). Keeping in view the stated cultural objective of these South Asian Nations, seven years back STAR News channel dumped the same News aired by BBC on which Beijing had objected, from its northern feed. On the sub continent Star takes an Indian centric line on News and Current Affairs even though its foot print extend several regions.

Thirdly, countries in the first stage of globalization tend to experience a wave of western programming; but in the second and the third waves of globalization, local versions of western programmes or genuinely local programmes become more visible. According to Anthony Giddens, Globalisation today is only partly westernization. Globalisation is becoming increasingly decentered not under control of any groups of nations, but of the large corporations. Its effects are felts as much in western countries as elsewhere. When audience appears to prefer locally made fare, the global media corporates globalise their production (glocalization). Sony has been at the forefront of this type of producing programmes with local companies in China, France, India and Mexico etc. This is also evident in the development of Al-Jazeera, the independent Qatar based Arab News channel as well as STAR TV and Zee TV in India and Phoenix TV in China. NDTV has produced the Indian version of the popular British hit serial "Yes Minister". In all these countries, there is a boom in local programming. UNESCO statistics in 1994 show that India and Korea now have the highest amounts of domestically produced television, about 92.0% of television programming. Indian viewers are most loyal to domestic programming

(99.0% of daily viewing) and Latin American produced telenovelas attract larger audience then American soap operas in Brazil and other Latin American countries. But western influence on television should not be underestimated, it is not as saturating as the proponents of cultural imperialism believe - and while there may be many American soaps filling in the dead times in the afternoon, they are not, in general, the most popular programmes.

Divya C. McMillian describes how the marriage of the global and the local is taking place in Indian television through hybrid programming in which western genres have been appropriated to fit different audience tastes and preferences. She had cited an example of a game show 'Adarsha Dampathigalu (The Ideal couple) telecast on regional TV channel 'Udaya', in which the audience anxiety over and enjoyment of the show are symptomatic of the uneasy articulation of the nation through the global and the local. The trend toward 'localizing the global' has happened also in talk shows, in News, and current Affairs (Al Jazeera in the Gulf, STAR in Asia) as well as the dubbing of nature programmes into local languages (i.e. National Geographic, Discovery and even some local productions on these channels) and of course the 24 hours movie channels showing archival Bollywood films. The marketing of the local in relation to the global can be seen in the rise of the 'Body shop', a successful 'multi local' corporation that promotes itself in the language of the global village. The 'Body shop' specializes in selling goods produced in specific third world locales to consumers through out the world. It emphasizes education and awareness of other cultures through the consumption of products that are made by others.

Another example can be cited of 'Sky Shop' telecast on different satellite channel.

Fourthly, due to cultural proximity with different countries in the region (J. Straubhaar, 2000), the impact and spread of cultural imperialism (in bad sense) has been minimised to a greater extent. It facilitate the exchange of programmes and create international market for media products, for example, programme once beamed among SAARC Nations under cultural programme exchange by Doordarshan. With the coming of transnational satellite, it has transformed the export trade in television from being the sale of broadcast rights of individual programmes scale and scope to their unique access to the largest market (Hoskins and McFadyen, 1991). Introduction of DTH system will speed up the process of globalization for India. Also these South Asian Communities having similar language and culture also generate substantial demand for Indian language programmes. To meet this demand many broadcaster such as Zee Telefilms Ltd.; B4U Television Network India Pvt. Ltd. and Sony Entertainment Television have set up operations abroad. For instance Zee TV has more than 30.0 million Viewers across 51 countries, DD-India (Now DD-world) also reaches to more than 50 countries in the world.

Globalization of television has its own negative aspects; i.e.,

(a) These media conglomerates, to a greater extent depends on advertisement revenue as they are commercial in their approach and attitude. This results in a preference for entertainment over controversy, serious political debate and discussions and documentries that dig deeply, inform, and challenge conventional opinion. There is more entertainment but little useful information. A survey conducted in the US during the Gulf war showed the more televison news coverage of the war people watched the less they new about the war and the more they supported the government policy. Advertisers would rather support media that put audiences in a passive, non-critical state of mind–making them easier to sell things.

(b) The very logic of private media market control and behaviour is antithetical to the cultivation and nurture of public sphere. Media outputs are commodified and are designed to serve market ends, not citizenship needs. Media, instead of encouraging political involvement, tend to strip politics of meaning and promote a broad depoliticization.

(c) The media have lost its diversity and the ability to present different points of view. Instead, there is homogeneity of news and a regurgitation of the same news stories on every channel and headline. Media conglomeration encourage popular tastes to become more uniform. Gerbner (1982) call it mainstreaming. He has argued that television blurs traditional social distinctions, blend otherwise divergent groups into the mainstream and bend the mainstream in the direction of the medium's interest in profit, populist politics and power. A multiplicity of TV channels is not an expansion of viewers' choice, it is an expansion of advertisers 'space (Deshpande, 1997) The values, beliefs, and practices of a few people are imposed on the audiences everywhere as if they are universal. Rupert Murdoch of the News corporation has tried to persuade the people that satellite television is a force for democracy, by passing totalitarian governments and beaming messages direct to the people. But the reality is that satellite business is a costly affairs and to make profit, accommodations have to be made with national governments, totalitarian or not (Bogart, 1994). In 1994 Rupert Murdoch's News corporation discontinued carrying BBC world service television channel in Asia because the Chinese leadership had objection over some programmes which may have hindered Murdoch's chance at the lucrative Chinese market.

There was a vision of benign 'global village' (McLuhan) is the 1960s where new technologies would allow an unlimited number of people to broadcast their own messages. This has not happened. Access to the hardware and marketing the product demands vast resources. Freedom once again loses out to finance. Forces resisting market domination are too few and too weak. Within the developing countries including India, citizen's resistance to domination of media market can hardly be seen except for the sporadic protests by some social activists and fundamentalist groups. Since media activism is still in its infancy it is difficult to say for sure what course it will take.

The basic lesson of television in India is that when global companies compete with national companies, the global often win. On the broadcast level there is no one who does not recognize the vast changes in the production of television culture that have taken place in India since 1991. Indian television has been totally transformed in the past 23 years (1982) since the launch of their national satellite, but the speed and the direction of that transformation has been affected by the first arrival of STAR TV's satellite signals and even more so by the presence of STAR as a leader in Indian television market today.

To understand globalization is to understand the sheer size of the top five or ten global entertainment and information companies. Among these companies there are a few, such as News Corp. and AOL Time Warner that control distribution systems (Satellite, Cable and the Internet) as well as content. Some have speculated in the past that the trend toward concentration would lead to just a few companies that would control much of our information and entertainment content that audiences receive and that trend has continued and promises to continue in the future. Size is the only one aspect of this phenomenon. In this context, treatment of content is also critical. Local or national interest donot and cannot dominate the thinking of global players whose concern is primarily economic and not political or cultural.

Indication is that Indian view globalization generally positively, in spite of the sociological problems linked to it, because of its open access to many cultures and communities. Global communication brings choice and diversity. The results of an opinion poll conducted by the 'Outlook' news weekly in early March' 2000 in six major cities across India reveals that 55.0 percent of those polled said, "American culture posed no threat to Indian culture, where as 33.0 percent said that it did. 58.0 percent supported the entry of multinationals in India, while only 29.0 percent were opposed to it". The case of India shows a new strategy for globalization of media production and distribution: a global corporation localizing content and becoming the primary source of national audience as Star has done recently.

There is also a degree of globalisation occuring in the media. Countries miles apart now share common images through the buying of programmes, from one television organisation by another.

Ironically, the challenge for many countries is how best to compete for their own domestic market with global companies. The struggle is not only economic but cultural. The question is, who should be responsible for creating the content for a cultural and political dialogue with a given audience through one of the most powerful medium available for reaching people? The answer lies in the hand of both policy makers and audiences in each country, but the dialectic of local versus global is being redefined by the outside forces.

Here I want to cite the quotation of Mahatma Gandhi that "I donot want my house to be walled in on all sides and my windows to be stuffed. I want the culture of all the lands to be blown about my house as freely as possible. But I refuse to be blown off my feet by any:". This become more relevant when it comes to culture and globalization. Today Indian television has become the mirror of cultural diversity present in the Indian society. Indian television in the era of globalization is witnessing the elimination of the government monopoly and the attempt at broadcasting regulation (as) mere reactions' (Mehta, 1998) due to technological development and market forces.

The real question is that whether urban Asian especially Indian family are adopting the American culture or Is the increasing preoccupation with sensate pleasure within segments of the urban middle class in India is also due to the influence of American media especially television or transformation due to globalization of television is taking place in the economy and social structure of the country. All these have to be taken into account while formulating policy by Indian policy makers then only can we utilise globalization of television and its impact in our favour.

References

- Rothschild, Emma: (1999), "Globalization and the Return of History," Foreign Policy, Summer.
- Scott, Margaret, "News from Nowhere", Far Eastern Economic Review (November. 28, 1991).
- Hyland, Mary, "Star Turns for young Murdoch, " Australian Financial
- Pathania, Geetika, "When Global Companies localize: Adaptive Strategies of Media Companies Entering India (Austin: University of Texas, Ph.D. dissertation, 1999)
- United States Department of Commerce, National Telecommunications and Information Administration (January 1993) Gobalization of Mass Media, Washington, General Printing office.
- Mac Bride, Sean, (1980), "Many Voices, One World", Paris, UNESCO.
- Bicket, Douglas, "Reconsidering Geocultural contraflow," Global Media Journal, Vol. - 4, Issue - 6, Spring 2005.
- Tomalinson, J. (1991), "Cultural Imperialism", Baltimore, MD: John Hopkins University Press.
- Mass Media in Society, (1996), St. Martin's Press.
- Blakley, Johanna "Entertainment goes Global: Mass Culture in Transforming World", Sponsored by Norman Lear Centre & Pacific Council on International Policy.
- Appadurai, A (1996), Modernity at Large: Cultural Dimensions of Globalization, University of Minnesto Press, Minneaspolis.

- Herman, E & R. MCchesney (1997): The Global Media: The New Missionaries of Global Capitalism, London.
- MCLuhan, M. "Understanding Media: In McQuail, D (1994) Mass Communication Theory, Sage, London.
- Boyd-Barrett O., (1998) Media Imperialism, Reformulated in Electronic Empires: Global Media and Local Resistance, Arnold, London.
- Khan, Habibul Haque (2004) Glocalization as Globalization: Evolution of a Sociological Concept, Journal of Sociology, Vol-1, No-2, Bangladesh.
- McMillian, Divya.C. (1999) "Identity and Consumerism on Television in India," University of Washington, Tacoma.

4

Globalization of Advertisement on Indian Television

Advertisement is any paid promotion of goods, services, companies and ideas by an identified sponsor. In general, advertisement is used to convey availability of a product and to provide information regarding that product.

If we look at the history of advertisement it can be traced back to the city of Babylon 500 years ago. They used symbols for this purpose, similarly ancient Egyptians used to carved messages on stone tablet and placed them along the main through-fares. In ancient Greek, Criers walked down the street shouting messages similar to television advertisements aimed at selling a particular product or services. Advertising agencies in modern world were first formed in Britain in the early 1800s. Today, all the above methods of advertising are still in use, though television, world over has emerged as the most effective media as it reaches not only due to its immense penetration across the greatest numbers of people and areas, but it also appeals to two of the most vital human senses - sight and sound. Television, today, has become the choice of advertisers, at least for those who could afford to launch a new product, initiate a promotion to boost up stagnant or decreasing sales.

There has been a long tradition of advertising in India since pre-Independence. In pre-Independence, ads; were mostly about ladies goods, gents clothes, travelling, eating places and entertainment for the British in India.

The foundation of professional advertising in India was laid by Jeweler Thompson and D.J. Keymer's, which was followed by others and B. Dattaram in 1907. Later on in the 1960s and 70s other Indian agencies also tried to carve out a place for themselves - ASP promoted by Birlas, the PSL by the Mahindras and Shilpi by the Sarabhais. ASP created a popular ads for Amul, i.e. 'Utterly Butterly Delicious - Amul". Radio services were also commercialized. Lintas started accepting accounts other than Lever, e.g., its campaign for 'Liril Soap' for Lever was not acceptable to the Lever team since it made bathing such a fantasy with a bikini clad model under a waterfalls, it was difficult to imagine that India's conservative society would accept such imagery. Since the year 2000 the same bikini clad models began to be accepted by the viewers due to globalization of Indian TV, for example, ads of 'Harry collection" suiting and shirting in which model speaks of her hottness following similar dress code.

It was in the 1960s and 70s that the concept of brand building appeared on the scene. 'Amul' and 'Made for each other' campaign are remarkable in this context. In 1976, Doordarshan became commercial and this brought a qualitative change in Indian advertising, later on with the opening of the economy in the 80s, there was a massive expansion in advertising in India with increased competition among multinationals and involvement of huge budget in it. Advertisers view India's as world largest market with its largest democracy as a commodity in the global market and television become a carrier to boost up their revenues.

The process of foreign satellite channels arrival in India was boosted by the liberalization and privatisation of the economy which begin in 90s. The first to enter in the Indian market was CNN, followed by STAR, Zee and a host of other channels. At present more than 100 satellite channels are operating in India. Globalization of television has ensured that the migrant communities of South Asians in the Middle East, Europe and North America became a new target as audiences and consumers. The entry of global media conglomerates has opened up a new visual world for Indian audiences. Buoyed by advertising revenue, cable and satellite television has increased their reach phenomenally, from 1.2 million homes in 1992 to 24.0 million homes. A total number of 91.0 million people comes under middle and upper middle class, as can be seen from the table given below: (which are their prospective buyers)

Household Income Distribution by Class*

Income group	Annual Income (Rs)	Annual Income (A$)	Urban ('000)	Rural ('000)	All India ('000)	No. of people (million)	Share of pop. (percent)
Low	<12500	625	14,895	68914	83,809	420	59
Lower Middle	12501-25000	625-1250	13,904	24,445	38,349	192	27
Middle	25001-40000	1250-2000	7,175	7,232	14,407	72	10
Upper middle	40001	2000-2800	2,591	1,191	3,782	19	2.6
High	>56001	>2800	1,505	552	2,057	10	1.4
Total			40,106	10,2335	142,441	713	

Note: *Estimated number of households by income group, 1989-90. Population figures are derived on the basis of an average household of 5 persons.

Source: National Council of Applied Economic Research (NCAER), *Consumer Market Demographics in India,* 1993.

Again satellite television has exposed consumers to global advertising and fuelled higher consumer ownership aspirations amongst the middle class and High Income Groups. Most of these media conglomerates (owing television) started in partnership with Indian broadcasting companies. Strategically, their Indian firms were programming and advertising sales units while unloading the library inventory on the new market allowed surplus revenue, cut down costs and optimized media products for the international networks. Even with limited market reach these global media have a niche in the urban or semi-urban middle class with significant purchasing power that advertiser are attracted to. The following table speaks about advertising companies working in India:

Table 4.1

Foreign Agency	Indian Agency
1) J Walter Thompson	Hindustan Thompson Association
2) Lintas World wide	Lintas India Ltd.
3) DDB Needham	Mudra Communication
4) Ogilvy Mather Worldwide	Ogilvy & Mather Ltd.
5) Euro RSCG	Ulka Advertising
6) D'Arey Macius Benton & Bowles	R.K. Swamy/BBDO Advtg. Pvt.
7) Dentsu	Rediffusion Advtg.
8) Young & Rubicom	Affiliation
9) Grey Advertising	Trikaya Grey Advertising
10) Saatchi & Saatchi	Everest Advtg. Pvt. Ltd.
11) Leo Burnett	Chaitra Leo Burnett
12) Mccann Erickson	Tara Sinha Mccann Erickson
13) Bozell Inc.	Arms Bozell

* Source: Market Report, NTDB, 17 August ' 1993.

In 1992, the top advertisers were Hindustan Lever, Tatas, Godrej, Proctor and Gamble, Parle, Colgate Palmolive, Nestle, ITC, Bajaj Auto and Philips. Six out of top ten advertisers were affiliated with the transnational corporations. This reflects an erosion in the local brands. Also fifteen of the twenty top advertising agencies have affiliations or joint ventures with the foreign agencies who are among the top international agencies and most of them are American in origin.

Foreign companies were seen to be initiating more aggressive advertising campaign and recent growth in advertising has been driven by television advertising especially the satellite channels, many of which are free to air, e.g., they relay for their revenue on advertisement (Sehgal, 2000). Besides this, the other factors which helped in growth of advertising in India's are :

(a) Foreign equity on advertising was removed in March' 2002. Foreign investors can now invest upto a maximum of 100.0 per cent equity through the automatic route, i.e., without prior approval from the RBI;

(b) With a huge middle class estimated between 200-300 million with aspirations to a western life style, with well linked satellite network, and

(c) Commercial guidelines rate card has been made advertiser friendly (Appendix-1)

'Advertising Age' claim that in 1993 the government lifted its ban on foreign advertisement on DD's five satellite channels, but still kept some of the ban on channel–One: ban on ads of alcohol. In 1994, DD lifted its ban on the advertisement of foreign products such as, Banks and Financial services and certain other products such as matrimonial agencies and hair dyes. The key products baned on DD is therefore, alcohol (Karnik Code), Cigarettes and tobacco. Products most advertised on DD's include cosmetics, soaps and detergents, while the satellite channels in 1997 tended to attract alcohol, consumer durables and expensive clothes. Audience Research Units of Doordarshan confirmed that 30.1 percent of advertising was for toiletries, and 21.1 percent was for food and Beverages. Consumer durable advertising was seen as educating for future consumer at that time (Bajpai & Unnikrishnan).

According to a McKinsey Report on India's consumption pattern, Indians have given up many of their traditional items used as soaps, shampoos or medicinal remedies, for example, charcoal-cleaned teeth are a rare sight, so is the case with twigs of Neem and Babul tree. Today the ultra bright shine of colgate or some other international brand of toothpaste holds more appeal than the traditional method of cleaning teeth. This is a clear cut indication of consumerism and globalization invading different parts of India. Similarly the Report says that the national advertisement spend on toilet soaps on Indian television has increased from Rs. 230 million in 1993 to Rs. 370 million in 1995. In the case of tea, the TV ads spend was Rs. 130.0 million in 1995 against just Rs. 75 million in 1993. Ad spends on tooth paste has doubled to Rs. 220 million in 1995 from Rs. 110 million in 1993. Slick advertising has definately played a major role in promoting the consumption of these items.

Gupta (1998), is of the view that there has been an exponential rise in advertising expenditure in India. This has resulted in advertising spending on television from 23.9 billion in 1996 to Rs. 49.0 billion in 2000. Out of which 25.0 percent was spent on the satellite channels in 2000 (Sehgal, 2000).

The ad-spend on television has grown at a compound annual growth rate of more than 30 percent over the past seven years, as against total ad spend which has grown at around 19 percent over the same period.

Table: 4.2 Ad-spend in India

(Rs. millions)

	1990	1991	1992	1993	1995	1998*	2000*
Total Advertising	15041	16400	18840	22270	37807	63538	86602
TV	2540	3170	3900	4630	11380	22520	30430
% TV of total	16.9	19.3	20.7	20.8	30.1	35.4	35.1

Source: Directory of Indian Television Industry '1996

*Projected figures

Indian Advertising

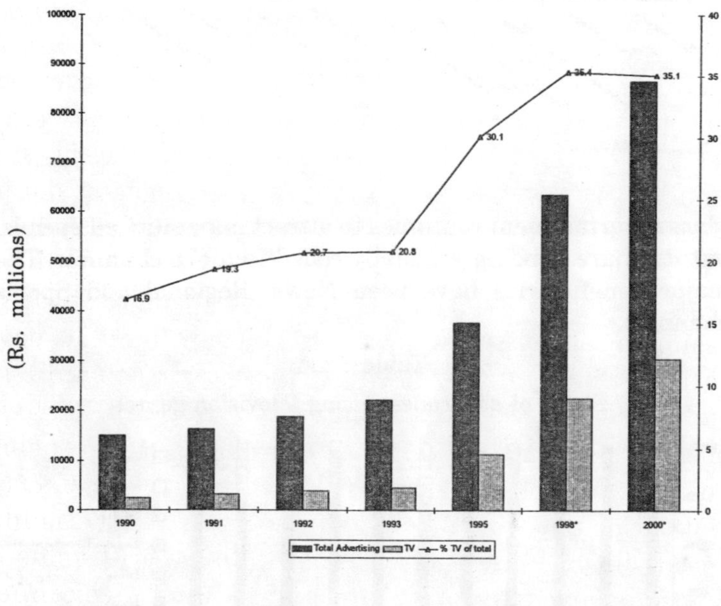

Advertising market soared from $ 37 billion to $ 58 billion between 1985 and 1995. Japan with 84.4% of market share top the position. The share of China and India is increasing significantly. The advertising market is buoyant and can see an increase of 75.0% between 1994 and 2003. Regarding expenditure on ads by the companies on Doordarshan, the diagram given below reveals the following facts:

Table : 4.3

Top Ten Spenders on television in 2004

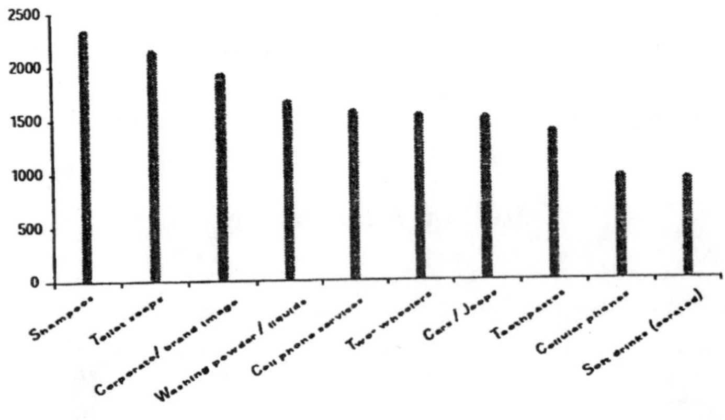

Source: TAM Adex

Mass entertainment continues to attract maximum ad spends, but its share is being gradually ceded to niche channels. The major beneficiaries have been News, Regional and Sports channels.

Table : 4.4

Share of advernues among television genres

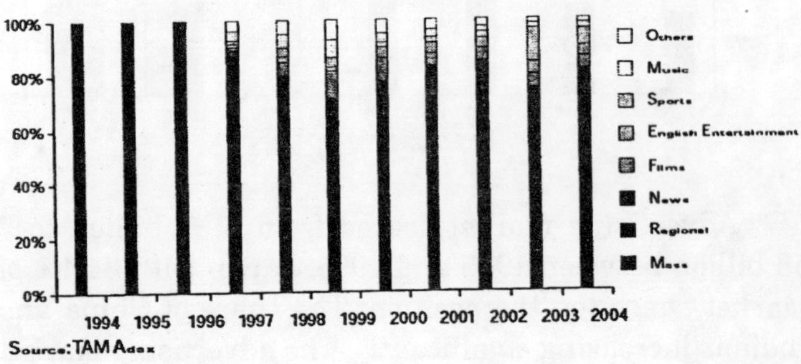

Source: TAM Adex

Similarly NCAER study which covered 515 cities and 182,599 Households in Urban areas reveals that the structure of the Indian society has an impact on the consumption patterns, which they further divided from very rich to destitute groups and accordingly they consume products of varying nature. Most of the respondents have television sets in their homes. How global advertisement has changed the consumption patterns of these groups can be viewed from the examples given below:

1) Honey: Previously it was available in plenty in the informal market, but after 1980s it was branded with Dabur and the impact is that corporate sector is reaping the reward instead of those working in informal sectors. This may lead to shortage and other problems in respect of this commodity.

2) Electric Rice Cooker: Rice is normally boiled in aluminium or stainless steel vessels or pressure cooker. In 1990s, Japanese electronics giant National introduced electric rice cooker, backed by aggressive advertising, promoting an easy life style. Now a large number of urban households are switching to this electric cooker. In 1993, at least 125000 electric cookers were sold and its sales will increase to 7-8 million units by the year 2000. It has increased demand for electricity as well as created problems of environmental pollution, which in turn has increased the demand of portable generators and invertors in Indian cities.

3) Baby Foods: Indian babies are usually breast-fed for upto 18 months and traditional cereal based foods are given from the age of six months. In

1989 a Swedish food processing multinational firm introduced its milk based cereals. It is major advertiser in both the electronic and print media. Now mother prefers to give this packaged food instead of preparing traditional cereal food.

4) Soft drink: A popular Indian thirst quencher is lime juice. In summer, it is sugarcane juice or plain water. But not any longer do Indians relay on their traditional thirst quencher with the entry of soft drinks like Coca Cola, Pepsi and others. And the market is also growing at the compound rate of 17.0 percent for these soft drinks.

5) Chocolates now marketed as a nutritious snack among adults besides sweet reward for children and this has increased its consumption in these years among different age groups. Now grown-ups and old donot feel guilt about eating chocolates.

By the late 1990s, multinational companies adopted certain methods to increase their advertisement

i) By customising their advertisement in the Indian market, for example, MTV brand customised its advertisement to suit the local tastes of the youths. Now special events like Valentine's Day, Mother's Day, Father's Day, Friendship day have been customised to suit Indians through global television which was previously unheard of except fews such as Teacher's Day (to show respect), but now the respect has been commercialized with the advent of satellite television; and

ii) Product endorsement by the celebrities and its association with the product to arouse national passion, such as cricket. The Korean company L.G.

sponsored the Indian cricket team in the world cup ' 2003 and 'Adidas' who had previously made their Indian ads in London, started making them in India in 1999 using Indian cricket star Sachin Tendulkar,. L'oreal increased its sales dramatically by using Miss India, who became Miss world, i.e. Diana Hayden alongwith its usual models (Fannin, 1999). This commodification of citizens was at its best during the Kargil war, when cricket stars, politicians, film and television personalities and other added glamour to the efforts to help the soldiers fighting on the border and the corporate ads lent an aura of emotional nationalism to the whole scene.

Thus global media flow has now penetrated everywhere and has been domesticated to suit specific Indian cultural specifities and preferences, for example, 'Kodak' successfully used the local idioms and culture to spread its message, i.e., through Kathakali dance and mask. Similarly 'Pepsi' Campaign used traditional festivals. In place of 'Taste the Thunder' slogan of Thumps up ad, now it has started with fresh campaign using the theme song "Sare Jahan Se Achcha, Hindustan Hamara'. It also depicts a material culture which play on the aspirations of a large middle class who are caught in the globalization process as they swing between their traditions and internalizing a transnational identity more in keeping with the global lifestyle. For example: Ad of 'Nokia' cellphone, which shows people belonging to different cultural groups incorporating enjoyable vision of cultural differences and lifestyles.

Overall advertising can be seen as one of the factors that contribute to shaping people's view of life and the basic values, attitude and cultural ideas that are dominant in society.

The advent of foreign advertisers in India has not always been successful and according to Sehgal, campaigns that failed in India includes Nike, Reebok, Johny Walker, Sony Panasonic, McDonald etc., and caused advertisers to look more closely at their strategy. One of the most dramatically insensitive campaign launched in recent years was that of cadbury-Schwepper, which compared its chocolate to Kashmir, i.e. "Too tempting, Too good to share", which cause a major outrage and had to be withdrawn (Economist, 2002). Now many of the foreign advertisers take caution while advertising their products through satellite television. For carrying out their business in India, they (a) Buy time slot on a channel which they feel has the highest penetration and enjoy maximum viewership for their target groups; (b) promote their products on the television during that time slot with the help of announcer/or motion picture depicting their usage and qualities. (c) Advertisers' must addresses local culture, value system and practices etc., in their advertisement for its success, meaning thereby, in place of globalization, Glocalization of products (advertisement) is the order of the day to succeed in the field of advertisement. (d) they have to maintain the ethical code of conduct, set up by the Advertising Standards Council of India, which is inspired by the Advertising Standard Authority of U.K. In the interest of the consumer and for fair advertising practice, ASCI follow the following guidelines:

- To ensure truthfulness and honesty of representations and claims made by advertisers and also to ensure against misleading advertisements.

- To ensure that advertisement are not offensive to generally accepted standard of public decency.
- To safeguard against indiscriminate use of advertising for promotion of products which are regarded harmful to the society or individual to a degree or type which is unacceptable to society at large; and
- To ensure that advertiser observe fairness in competition.

besides the above code of conduct, DD has its own code for commercial advertising which also put restrictions on unhealthy advertising, harmful to the society (Appendix-2).

Keeping in view the advertisers commercial approach who overlooks viewers interest and the ASCI and DD's code of conducts which are not abserved in toto to protect their interest, most countries have adopted some kind of regulations on their own for advertisement. As in Korea and Japan, advertising control is only for the free to air channels. In countries like 'Taiwan' and 'Thailand', advertising is banned on pay TV, while in Canada it is banned on pay and premium channels. In the USA, this restriction is only for children's programmes, in Sweden and Norway, TV ads and sponsorship of programmes aimed at children below 12 years are prohibited. Some research studies reveals that some children understand the purpose of advertising that appears on TV as early as 5 years of age but in most cases it is 12 years and above (38.0%). If the children do not understand the underlying purpose of advertising, it is likely that they will not question the message it conveys and will easily become prey in the hand of advertisers'. In Greece, ads of toys on TV is banned between 7.00 am and 10.00 pm. In

Germany and Denmark, there is ban on certain forms of toys. In Austria and some part of Belgium, no ads is permitted five minutes before or after programmes for children.

In this context an experiment was conducted in Norway that how advertisement plays with the values and wants of younger children. The study was conducted among children and parents in two day nurseries in two towns with a similar social structure, one having access to satellite TV and commercials and another without it. The study revealed that the parents were under strong pressure to buy the children's play toys which was more dominated by those launched in various promotional contexts at the nursery in the town with satellite TV and commercials than in the other nursery without it.

But in India, free to air channels are currently 100.0 percent reliant upon advertising and pay channels about 70.0 percent on an average, thereby implying that advertising revenue is the primary source of funding for the industry and investment in new and existing programming. This is contrary to the experience of most mature global cable and satellite markets, where there is an even balance between advertising and subscription. In India there are no channels which relay entirely on the subscription revenue. On the contrary market only has channels which either relay on advertising revenue or both. 'HBO' for instance which generate revenue from subscription in the USA has changed business practice for Asia and is viewed only as a premium movie channel in the advanced economy. It is a basic tier channel in Taiwan and Philippines but partially reliant on advertising in India because of low monthly per subscriber revenue.

An analysis of television programming indicates that advertising in India, on an average, amounts to 192 seconds (3.2 minutes) per hour. It is still significantly lower than several other countries. Of course, in the case of prime time for mass entertainment channels, this number could go as high as 600 seconds (10 minutes).

International norms on ad clutter

The norms and standards for the amount of advertising that can be shown on television vary from country to country. TAM Media Research has compiled an illustrative list of standards, some of which are mentioned below:-

- Australia Broadcasting Authority recommends 10 minutes of advertising per hour for children's programming and up to 15 minutes for non -prime programmes.
- Philippines stipulates a commercial load for television in Manila to 18 minutes per hour, while for provincial television stations, commercial load permissible is a maximum of 20 minutes per programme hour.
- In China, a maximum of 9 minutes of ad time per hour of programming is allowed.
- Canada recommends 8 minutes of advertising per hour for children's programming and 12 minutes per hour for other programming.
- The average for other Asian countries is around 8 minutes of ad time and 2 minutes of programme promotion time, i.e. a total of 10 minutes of break duration per hour.

Table: 4.5

Pure advertising time for every hour of programming in India

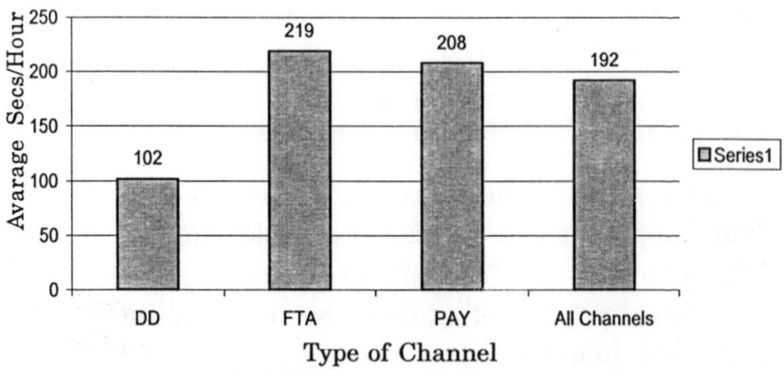

Source : TAM Media Research

Despite prevailence of different organisations, such as ASCI, DD's code, C&S Regulation Acts enacted by TRAI and a hosts of other regulations adopted by different countries regarding advertisement on global television, sociologists and anthropologists have complained that advertising barges into the homes with pseudo-populist rhetoric that in fact encourages a starkly materialistic approach to the world and promotes an ethos suggesting that what one posses is more important than who one is. This lead to imitation of the elite by the poorer sections of the society and devoting their limited resources to ape a lifestyle well beyond their reach and further compromising with their quality of life (Mankekar). In other word, it creates 'conspicuous consumption' of the leisure class as Veblen has conceptualized. Increase materialism results in tearing of the social fabrics. Consumer advocates have further accused advertisement for victimizing children. All these and other gimmicks leads to cropping up of different problems in social life creating host of socio-economic and other dysfunctional activities. Some of these are described below to have an insight into the advertisement on global television.

Vilanilam has observed that television advertising in India presents a heterogenous cross-section of the Indian population with images of products and life styles that are economically out of reach for the vast majority. In this way advertising constitutes an imaginary world of desire that addresses not only the elites who can purchase such goods and in doing so affirm their elite status, but for the masses of Indian populance and poor for whom the imaginaire is merely a reference point, a shaper of aspirations, an ideal model of success, pleasure and envy.

These images of products are repeatedly advertised on television for its long lasting effect. In some instances, an advertiser will put forth the perfect image of a lifestyle using the right symbols to which the viewers will aspire and the product will be seen by the viewers as a necessary component. So regardless of the kind of life style actually led by the viewers, the advertisers succeed in getting himself projected what he wants. And because the product is a part of the picture, the viewer also buy the product, which shows that "symbolic interactionism" is at work and it also help in shaping the world view cultivated in audiences, because viewers get heavy doses of television viewing which leads to a false perception of affluence in them (0'Guninn and Shrum, 1997). McMillin (2003) adopting cultivation approach has found that television influences clothing, food and other consumption practices. According to McMillin, television plays an important role in cultivating and sustaining the ideology of capitalism many a times referred to as

Americanisation in western parlance and asserts that television in India has played a crucial ideological role in sustaining these impoverished positions throughout the nation's in the post colonial period.

Television advertising is seen to play on the foreign obsessions of many Indians since 1990s, significantly increasing their desires for advertised products which started the beginning of cultural imperialism. But many viewers no longer identify with the advertised products set up in the backdrop of well equipped, affluent middle and upper middle higher classes, which has no relevance for the vast marginalised people of the country. It also creates its own images of beauty, family life, lifestyle, concept of branded items compatible with consumer culture and conspicuous consumption. Under such impact of globalisation, the appearance of women in advertisement in India has changed the notion of Indian beauty which has taken a westernized turn, making the traditional images of beauty outdated and out of sync. (Helped by Miss India/World such as Sushmita Sen, Aishwarya Ray, Diana Hayden etc.). Ad of 'Elle-18' says to every woman consumer: Because you are worth it. Similarly a 'De Beers' ad shows a girl saying @ I wasn't born a princess, but my father turned me into one. On the family front, a population so far nurtured by the ideals of the Ramayana and the Mahabharata is now being made to see a globalized version of a family. A young brother is being shown in a shampoo ad attached to his equally lively sister through a shampoo pouch. Besides these ads, there are many other ads which shows that global advertisement has changed Indians' images about their culture and traditions.

In Kasser's opinion, the unrelenting message through advertisement is that consumption and possession represents the only two routes to lasting fulfillment. The materialism that global television directly shapes has been found to be deeply dysfunctional. One associated with depression, anxiety, insecurity, physical illness, social isolation, lack of empathy and a general dissatisfaction with life. The consumer it cultivates become maximally greedy, wholly oblivious and ultimately harmful to the collective interest.

In the course of Rahul Prebisch Lecture at Belgrade on 8th June, 1983, the then Prime Minister (Late) Smt. Indira Gandhi spoke that "transnational advertising arouses new desires which distort economic priorities and lure people into artificial consumption patterns". Asian Advertising (1980) reports that commercial advertisement was discontinued on Indonesian television from 1981 because of its socially destabiling effect through the generation of wants not matched by the means of satisfying them. This indicate how advertising will have its effects on different sections now-a-days when global television has entered most of the homes.

Marcuse (1968) is of the opinion that the system of indoctrination unleased by the media-advertising nexus manipulates people and create false needs among them. Chomsky (1989) extending the argument of Marcuse further asserts that consumers are like product which are sold by manipulating media to a willing buyer by private media corporations. This manipulation is achieved through the creation and control of images and representation by media. Hirschman & Thompson (1997) have observed the symbiotic relationship between advertising and programming and suggested that programmes have a greater advertising impact because of lower level of viewers skepticism.

Globalization has led to replacement of the existing cultural common sense (Gramsci) of the local communities by an ahistorical cultural commonsense. Ahistorical because the umbilical chord of the elements of the traditional cultural commonsense have been ruptured by the unrelented elements belonging to different contexts under the compulsions of globalization. How the global advertisement has influenced local culture can be seen in the 'coca cola' ads, shown on different channels. In this ad, young boys are shown playing cricket in streets. Nusrat Fateh Ali, the late famous urdu Quawali singer from Pakistan is singing in the background. Red chillies are being dried under scorching sun (coca cola is also associated with red colour). Agra's Taj Mahal is also being shown alongwith small girls performing classical dance. Seen this way, ad seek to promote a product by rupturing the cultural commonsense and creating a new image for the product to gain acceptance. Similarly the forces of globalization while creating a world based on the false sense of individuality have nothing to do with the betterment of the social milieu that would guarantee equal opportunities to all irrespective of one's purchasing capacity. The political economy of globalization in a hierarchical society like India is bound to aggravate the inegalitarian system rather than uplifting the sections of population having no access to resources and technology. The 'complan' ad creates such individual identity (in India) where at least half of the total population donot have access to proper diet.

Fiske and Hartley have noted that advertising doesnot represent the 'manifest actuality' of the society but rather symbolically reflect the social values. The researchers pointed out that advertising insists on an idealized goal of achieving personal happiness, success and security and it does this by first depicting a world over represented by young, beautiful, successful and happy-wealthy people and then creating a desire in the audience to better their lives or to achieve the desirable attributes of the people as shown in the advertisement and finally it portrays the product as a bridge toward achieving the goals, for example, different products having tag with Amitabh Bachchan, Sachin Tendulkar, Sushmita Sen, Aishwarya Ray and host of other Indian celebrities comes under this category. Again in order to attract and hold the attention of the potential consumers and create a favourable attitude toward the product, advertising must reflect the cultural values and norms of the society. Therefore, it is possible to gain an insight into the current social values and norms by analyzing the structures of meaning found in advertisement, for example, the ad of 'Raymond' involving traditional ceremony of marriage reflects Indian cultural values and the changing family image implying changing Indian social values.

According to Sanbonmatsu and Fazio, if an advertisement is placed in programme of similar nature or content, it will be remembered better than if it is placed in a programms with wholly dissimilar content. For example, an advertisement for a home decorating product such as 'Asian Paint' by Amitabh Bachchan, would be expected to be more memorable if placed in a programme of differing thematic content (as, about cars).

Howard argues that high involvement programmes (such as, Ramayana, Mahabharata and other serials, film based/films, sports like cricket etc.) results in poorer recall of advertisements because of viewers' annoyance at having a programme with which they are involved got interrupted. The negative relationship between recall and involvement is explained theoretically as an effect of cognitive intereference. Norris and Colman, (1993) referred to the limited capacity of the human information-processing system and argued that if a programme is highly involving, viewers find it difficult to switch their attention from it to adjacent or embedded advertisements, resulting in poorer recall of the advertisment.

In 1991, Srikandath studied the values depicted in Indian television advertising and concluded that the main values being promoted were technology, modernisation and consumerism. Bajpai and Unikrishnan found that television is playing a significant role in the expansion of consumer values in Indian society. Children are effectively being groomed to become future consumer and that values were being promoted supporting individualism and nuclear family. But the late Stig Carlson, former DG of the EACA was of the view that advertising doesnot change or create new values instead of that it detect new values among consumers which is reflected in their creative solution. Advertising is thereby instrumental in bringing new products and their attributes to the attention of the public. It has also given boost to India's industries and its economy by creating competition for the products so that viewers (consumers) could be benefited out of it. How much of the growth is influenced by advertising?, the International Development Research Centre of Canada has attempted to find this out among children in Delhi in early 1996. The results were revealing. Almost 75.0% of children in the age group of 8-15 yrs said that they want to own products advertised on television. Asked to name their ten favourite ads, they named detergent and even airline ads rather than those of toys, games, sweets or food products.

Another study conducted by the NCAER (February. 1996) states that there are over 900 million Indians, out of which 780.0 million uses cooking oil, over 760 million are tea consumers, 450 million buyers are of casual footwear, 40 million own TV sets, two and a quarter million owns automobiles etc. And most of them are buyers of advertised products on TV.

The thing about advertising is that it picks up a trend and builds it into a movement. It is a mirror of society which is corraborated with the finding of above studies.

In the end we can ponder on, "Is Indian advertising globally relevent ? can we able to create a world class advertising ? In the sponsored" Crossfire" seminar held in Mumbai on August 17, the participants had tried to answer these question. According to them, the content must be relevant to the audience and adopting this formula, MTV has succeeded and beaten channel [V]. Economic condition is also favourable for the globalization of the Indian advertising industry. Already most of the top agencies have tied up with international agencies and with more liberalization, it seems that there will be more cross-border exchange of peoples and ideas. And then there is India itself as a brand value. As J. Philip Jones stated that "of course there are differences between an Indian and a western audience, but there are a lot more similarities because advertising deals with emotions and it is universal.".

Stringent measures and devices have to be adopted by the Government of India in association with different NGOs as well as advertising associations working in India to stop the ill effect of global advertisement which has increased conspicuous consumption and also distorted Indian culture as Pollay viewed advertising as a 'distorted mirror' reflecting certain underlying values and life styles, which in turn affect culture. Before airing advertisement on television, its contents should be analysed and if something is found wrong, it can be modified or stopped. The advertiser should also take into account the current social values and norms while formulating their advertisements. As discussed, most of the global advertisers' including Indian prohibits such programming which lacks in creating proper understanding about their products pros and cons. For this programme like 'Lo Aaa Gaye Satyamma' for 'Jago Grahak Jago' telecast on DD-1 channel is in right direction creating awareness among viewers (consumers). Such type of programming on different channels will certainly put moral pressure and will act as a detterent factor for advertiser's who donot bother about their viewers (consumers). Besides this, recommendation of TRAI on advertisement should be implemented, which is as follows:

(i) There should not be any regulation, at present, on advertisement on both FTA and Pay channels.

(ii) The Cable Act should be suitably modified so that powers are available with the government to regulate this if found necessary at a later stage. Broadcasters would also be required to give information on advertising time to TRAI and the Government. This would also be made available to the public through the TRAI web site.

(iii) Broadcasters should be free to decide which channel should be FTA and which should be pay.

Report of the working group on software for DD's in which suggestion regarding commercial advertisements have been made is relevant even today. According to expert report, it should be area-specific because advertisement of such products which are not found in those parts of the country where it is advertised will create destabiliging effect ultimately leading to frustration. Similarly, advertisement of luxury consumer goods by transnational television has led to increase in corruption in the society, which should also be looked into for society's benefit. OM dated 16.7.2001 in this respect is appended in the Appendics.

References

- Ahmed, N. Article on Cross-cultural content Analysis of Advertising from US and India.
- Appadurai, A., 1996, "Modernity at Large: Cultural Dimensions of Globalization, Minneapolis, University of Minnesto Press.
- Advertising: World Federation of Advertisers, 2002, EACA & UNEP.
- Tej Bhatia, Advertising in Rural India; Language, Marketing, Communication and Consumerism; Institute for the study of Languages and Culture of Asia and Africa, 2000, Tokyo Press, Tokyo, Japan.
- Business World Marketing White Book, 2003-04.
- Bajpai, S. & Unnikrishnan, N. " 1996, 'The Impact of Television Advertising on Children, Sage Publications, New Delhi.
- Basu, Aparimita, "Thesis Paper on Media Laws: An Overview.

- Bjurstrom, Erling, 1994, "Children and Television Advertising, Konsument verket (Swedish Consumer Agency).
- Ciochetto, Lynne; 2004 "Advertising and Globalization in India", Massey University, Wellington, New Zealand.
- Chatterjee, P.C., 1991 "Broadcasting in India", Sage Publication, New Delhi.
- CUTS, Sustainable Consumption series, 1999, Camac Street, Calcutta. No. 1, "Advertisement and Consumption....'.
- Chomsky, Noam, 1989 "Necessary Illusions: Thought Control in Democratic Societies," South End Press, Boston.
- Directory of Indian Television Industry, 1996, India.
- Dasegowdanakoplu, P., 2004 "Expanding Media Market and Shrinking Public Sphere, Mangalore University, Karnataka.
- Daniel A. Pope, 1983 "The Making of Modern Advertising.
- Economist: Sticky Issue, 24 August' 2002.
- Gupta, Nilanjana, 1998, "Switching Channels: Ideologies of Television in India", Oxford University Press, Delhi.
- Griffin, M., Global Media Journal: Fall 2002, Vol. 1 "Cultural Imperialism to Transnational Commercialization".
- Harris, Grey. 1984, "The Globalization of Advertising, "International Journal of Advertising, Vol. 3.
- Jena, S.K. 2000, "Globalization & Popular Culture: Reading Advertisements Sociologically (Seminar paper: JNU and Albert Ludwigs University, Freiburg).
- Janus, N. 1984. "Transnational Advertising: The Latin American case". In World Communications: A Handbook, (ed.) G. Gerbner & M. Siefert, Longman, New York.
- Kasser, T., 2002 "The High Price of Materialism". Bradford Books/ MIT Press, Cambridge.

- McKinsey Quarterly Report: Media and Entertainment, Various Issue.
- McDonald, R., 2003 "Finding Happiness in Wisdom and Compassion —The Real Challenge for an Alternative Development Strategy". Journal of Bhutan Studies, 9.
- McMillin, Divya. C. 2003 "Television, Gender, and Labour in the Global City". Journal of Communication, (53) 3, (496-511).
- O' Guinn Thomas C., & Shrum, L.J. 1997, "The Role of Television in the Construction of Consumer Reality", Journal of Consumer Research (23) 4, (278-294).
- Page, David & Crawley, William, 2001, Satellite Over South Asia: Broadcasting, Culture and the Public Interest, Sage Publications, Delhi.
- Rai University: Ethics in Advertising: ASCI Code for Commercial Advertising on DD, Indian Advertising" (Lesson-19).
- Robert Goldman, 1992, "Reading Ads Socially", Routledge, London.
- Suresh, N. 1996,, "Consumer Unity and Trust Society, paper on sustainable consumption, 3-B, Camac Street, Calcutta.
- Sanskriti (Magazine), Issue 2 Oct., 1996, No. 1, vol-7 article by S. Rao, The Selling of Global Cultural Difference.
- Sehgal, R., 2000, "Sunny Skies Aread for Indian Channels".
- Srikandath, S., 1991, "Cultural Values Depicted in Indian Television Advertising", International Journal of Mass Communication Studies.
- TRAI Recommendation on Issues relating to Broadcasting and Distribution of TV Channels, 1st October 2004, Govt. of India, N. Delhi, (Section:-8: Advertising).
- Thussu, D.K. "Indian Media: From Colonial to Global", University of North London, England.

- -------------------"Taming the Dragon and the Elephant: Murdoch's Media in Asia.
- Werner Vom Busch (ed.), 2004, "The Asia Media Directory", Konrad-Adenauer Foundation, Singapore.
- Vilanilam, J. 1989 "Television Advertising and the Indian Poor", Media, Culture and Society, London.
- A. Furnham J. Bergland and Barrie Gunter, 2002, Memory for Television Advertisements as a Function of Advertisement Programme Congruity in Applied Cognitive Psychology, John Wiley & Sons, Ltd.

5

Globalization of Contents and Indian Television

Globalization and technological progress has given consumers worldwide access to a multitude of entertainment and information services on the one hand, and on the other side, it has also made the domestic cultural industries more vulnerable to foreign competition. The growth of multinational corporations and vertical integration of entertainment, distribution, delivery systems and cultural products are making it increasingly difficult for many countries to protect their cultural diversity which forms the basis of their sovereignty and identity.

This expansion also demanded new programmes content – from News to game and Chat Shows, from Soap Operas to Reality TV which have been provided by a burgeoning television industry that is increasingly going global.

It has also brought forth a new set of values including broadcasting values. The concept of global village has now been transformed into a global market where the transnationals are main sellers of their cultural products and informations. Keeping in view, such situation, now the Indian content producing countries are also exploring the possibilities of co-productions with renowned international players, (viz; Zee, STAR etc.)

As these companies are aware that satellite broadcasting is a market operation where cultural products are looked upon as a commodities which can bring in profits to the investors and this ultimately depends on the contents of the programmes telecast on global television which may be factual, as in documentaries, news and reality television or fictional as in comedy and drama. It may be topical as in the case of news and some made for television movies or historical as in the case of documentaries on fictional series. It may be instructional as in the case of education programme or entertainment or sitcom, reality TV and variety show. Further it can be categorised under two headings: (a) International content aspect; and (b) local content aspect. Now the global satellite television has adopted two strategies, keeping in mind both the content aspects, in prepairing cultural products for global markets, i.e., (a) Global localization or glocalization; in this process the global genres are adapted for local audience so that global blends with the local, for this Robertson has discussed various ways; and (b) Negotiated modification: In this process, carefully selected national cultural products, such as, TV serials are globalized by editing or revising them to suit the tastes of the consumers in other countries whose taste donot conform to those of consumers in the country of origin (Bielby & Harrington, 2002). In this regard, D.K. Thussu, writes that "the processes of negotiation are more complex and this is evident in the way the west has had to adapt to Indian condition exemplified by the growth of Indian made programmes in its languages and broadcast on foreign owned satellite channels". In other word, it has been Indianization of American formats which created a new model of hybridization between the east and the west. This process further went on with regionalization and finally localization of global programming to suit the range and variety of cultural and linguistic tastes encompassing the Indian market. One major outcome of this media marriage is the development of "Hinglish", the language of international media. The cloning of American programmes has been done by most of the global television working in India, for example, Sony Entertainment TV has cloned 'Charlie Angels', under the name of 'CATS'. The news on Star TV resembles that of BBC, and it even has a programme which imitates the latter's interview show "Hard Talk". The sitcom "Friend" telecast on STAR world has an Indian version called "Hello Friends" telecast on STAR Plus. Another programme telecast on STAR Plus is "KBC", which is a clone of "Who Wants to Be a Millionnaire". Apart from American format now Indian television has moved to other centres of cultural production, which include in its gambit telenovelas from Brazil and Mexico, Islamic soap operas from Egypt and Turkey, films from China, India, Iraq and Senegal, cartoons and serials from Japan, International News from Dubai and Saudi (i.e. Al Jazeera TV), some of these cultural production has been cited here: A popular Chinese serial dubbed in Hindi, i.e. 'Himgiri ke Veer' has already been telecast on Doordarshan and Zee TV, 'Oshin' a Japanese serial became very popular in Iran and India. Serial 'Jassi Jaisi Koi Nahin' telecast on Sony is an adaptation of Latin American soap called "Betty La Fea". Despite all these, mostly western countries dominated the global television market with its content such as, "Surf wheel of Fortune", modelled along the lines of the American "Wheel of Fortune", Zee TV "Highlife" closely resembles the 'Life styles of the Rich and Famous' of CNN, 'Swabhimaan', telecast on Doordarshan was modelled along the line of "The Bold and the Beautiful".

Global television has undoubtedly affected local programmes and its genres like the news show/bulletin, the soap operas, the sitcom and the game show. Local version of these genres are often no more than poor imitations. At the same time local language channels have developed indigenous genres such as those based on Indian film songs. The best example of this is the musical programme called "Chhaya Geet". Another genre which has been indigenously developed is the religious epic such as "The Mahabharata", "Ramayana", "Srikrishna" and others.

All the above programme genres speaks about the philosophy of the contents, be it foreign or its local version and to some extent its impact on other cultural products of the countries where it takes place. In this context, Joshi (1998) is of the view that the contents of television programmes are dependent not so much on the country of origin as the philosophy or identity that the channel wants to preserve for itself. The foreign programmes transmitted on Doordarshan has a distinct identity of their own. They are more in consonance with the over-all socio-cultural conditions of the country.

Foreign transmission on some other channels are either neutral to the local country conditions or they are insensitive to them. Doordarshan, for example, has defined for itself a social philosophy or objective which insists that its prorammes works as a catalyst for social change, stimulates scientific temper, aim towards social welfare of women, children and less privileged, create value of appreciation for arts and cultural heritage alongwith entertainment. This means that whether programme telecast are of Indian origin or foreign origin, they have to confirm to the social objectives. But critics are of the view that in present scenario, in response to the new competition from global broadcasters, DD has changed its contents accordingly. As can be seen in the diagram given below:

Genrewise Viewership Share in 2004 (In percentage)

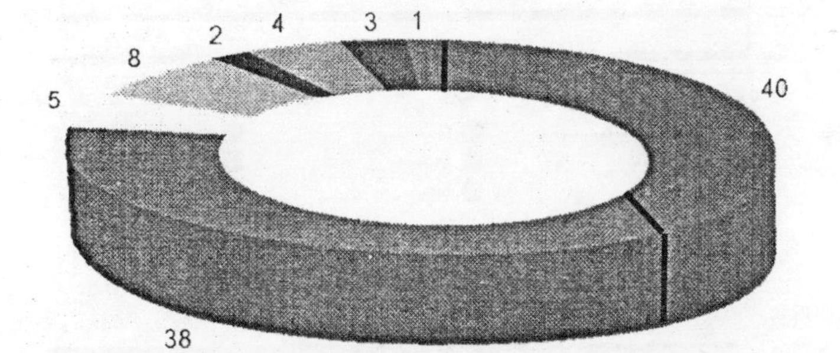

Source: TAM Media Research

In this process, some of the basic objectives stated above have been ignored, such as the basic requirements of the public service, as stated by Andrew Graham's 'merit goods'. It is ironic, however, that in reflection of India's cultural diversity, some of the global satellite channels currently have a stronger claim to success than Doordarshan, particularly in the south and more recently elsewhere satellite channels are providing space for regional cultures on a far greater scale than the national broadcaster.

Regional channels have been Jostling for viewership in the face of increasing quality and variety of offering by mass channels, and the emerging popularity

Table : 5.1

Viewership pattern across locations

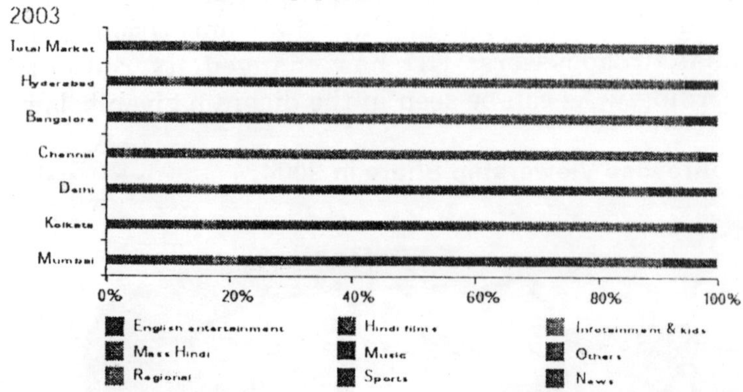

Table : 5.2

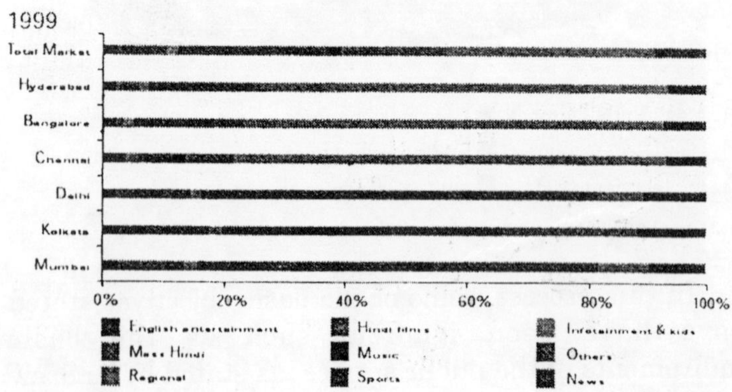

Source: TAM Media Research

of niche channels. In West Bengal, Maharashtra and the four Southern States i.e; Andhra Pradesh, Karnataka, Kerala and Tamil Nadu, though, consumers have continued to establish a definite demand for regional content. However, this space is characterised by low ad rate realisations, low production budgets, and "me too" programming and fierce competition between various channels.

The large regional variations necessitate the need for a more targeted and segmented approach for content, in an addressable scenario.(CII- KPMG Report on Media)

Besides this some satellite channels are serving specific purpose of the audiences, such as, 'Discovery' is devoted to environment, culture, science, wildlife etc., and work as enrichment channel. BBC world or CNN are devoted to News and current affairs channel. They also strive for profit but within the boundaries defined for themslves. But all channels do necessarily have such a philosophy or objectives for themselves. In a recent study by the Euromedia Research Group, Dennis Mcquail discusses a range of research that went into content changes and notes that it produces a rather unclear picture. In some countries, public service broadcasters are still keeping to their remit, in others they would appear to have acquired a marked reliance on the entertainment function.

Besides content, there has been marked shift in the format of the global entertainment trend. Traditionally most international formats were created in the USA and subsequently produced around the world using the American model. This can be seen in the worldwide spread of traditional formats, such as, "family Feud', 'The Price is Right' and 'Wheel of Fortune'. On the other hand, in most of the developing and third world countries, pro-development issues find prominent place in different programmes such as 'Buniyad', 'Humlog', Jasoos Vijay, 'Kalyani (telecast on regional DD channel) etc. telecast on Doordarshan. There is a marked difference between traditional soaps and pro-development soaps and other programmes based on it, which is as follows:

Traditional Soap operas	Pro-development soap operas
Entertainment	Entertainment & Education
Value erosion	Value Reinforcement
Morally incoherent	Morally coherent
Unrealistic	Realistic
Atheoretical Development	Theoretical Development
Produced mostly in the United States	Produced mostly in the Third World.

However, over the past five years, there has been a geographical shift in the origin of the international formats with countries such as the Netherland, and the UK, now accounting for the creation of many of the successful entertainment shows. Titles, such as, 'The weakest link', "Test the Nation', 'Dog Eat Dog', "The Mole", Who Wants to be a Millionnaire', and of course 'Big Brother', have all been developed within Europe before travelling to an international audience. In the international television market of today, there are fewer cultural exceptions to a successful format and increasingly broadcasters are chasing the same 'Must have' Key show to fill up their schedules. The global success of hit formats such as 'Big Brother', "Screentime Popstars' etc.; telecast in over 20 countries proves that viewer tastes are becoming increasingly similar, no matter where in the world they live. Also in the lines on similar pattern are', "Indian Idol' "Kaun Banega Crorepati' etc. an adaptation of American reality show (game show). Infact, programme format adaptation is a feature of most of the television market in Asia. Despite the negative connotations of cloning or copying, the practice of adapting television format is taking place all over the world, as it includes emulation, hybridization and localization of programme format. In this context, Lee (1991) has studied the influence of foreign programme in shaping programme formats in recipient countries, which is more subtle and varied. Also the absorption and indigenization of foreign cultural products vary depending on the extent to which they absorb the form and content of foreign cultures. These have been categorised into four patterns:

(a) Amoeba Pattern: which keep the content and not the form (i.e.; game show).

(b) Parrot Pattern: wholesome adaptation of foreign format (cloning effect).

(c) Corral pattern: which keep the form but change the content (i.e., foreign melodies with local lyrics)

(d) Butterfly pattern: which absorbs and indigenizes foreign culture to an extent that one can hardly distinguish the foreign from the indigenous, for example, films of Satyajit Ray having unique confluence of western technology and Indian culture.

Chat show, game show, Leisure programmes and quiz contests are some other examples of hindi adaptation of western formats. MTV is also an example of multilocal format. There are ten variants of MTV in Asia, mostly on a nation specific basis like MTV India. It has adapted international show 'Road Rules' for local Indian market as 'MTV Roadies' and US video music award in form of 'IMMIES'. All these indicates that there is a strong demand for ethnic programmes in India and keeping in view MTV India success, some other channels have also reoriented their programmes to cater specifically to the Indian taste. Some of the satellite channels which have adapted itself to Indian culture and its audience tastes are ZEE, STAR TV, Sony Entertainment etc.

As stated above, Asian and especially Indian audience expresses preference for regional programmes, in local, national languages because they feel it easier to identify with the style, values, attitude, and behaviour expressed in local programmes than in foreign programmes (Biltereyst, Chadha & Kavoori). This is known as cultural discount. The trend toward localization or regionalization of media content is partly a result of the cultural relevance or proximity brought by the audience. In this regard, two trends are worth mentioning: (a) the growing hybridization of media languages and the (b) popularity of channels and programming format, which has been indigenized from foreign models. This partially explains the success of the Indian channel ZEE TV; whose 75.0 percent programmes are local in origin. Similarly STAR TV has been able to localise content in India due to availability of indigenous programming. As the Indian entertainment industry is one of the biggest industry with annual turnover of almost $ 425 million. So most of these channels get enough material from this industry. The Asian Business News channel cater to the demand of specific region. Other international broadcastes are adapting their programmes to the cultural, political and linguistic diversity of the region. Also in order to overcome language obstacles and increase their audience, global satellite television are investing increasingly in national language, example of such global television in India are: CNN, NBC, STAR TV to name a few among hosts of other global satellite channels. Regarding hybridization, Zee TV in particular has met with huge success through its adaptation of general entertainment formula to the Hindi language, a process which has been known as Hindigenization. However, both the popularity and the content of these new Hindi language entertainment channels, according to David Page and William Crawley, has given rise to apprehensions that the culture of Bollywood is swamping other national cultures and even destroying the ideological boundaries of the Nation State. Perhaps this is due to increase in films and film based telecast on most of the Hindi channels operating in India. Even though the percentage of socially relevant programmes of the national broadcaster declined to accomodate entertainment of a hybrid variety but their is an ideological shift in television culture, i.e.; from public service to profit oriented programming reflecting the growing commercialization of the medium with market forces dominating the broadcasting agenda in India. This can be seen from the programme composition of DD-India (2003), an international channel. 42.0 percent of the total share in programming consists of entertainment, music and serials.

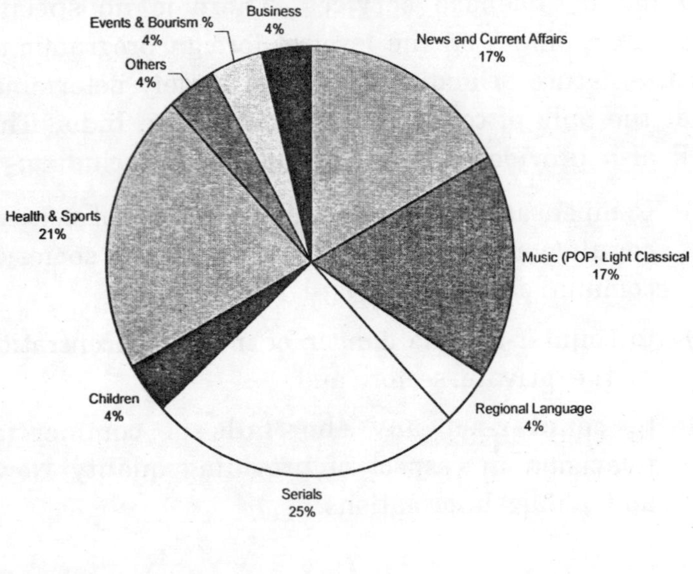

This may be due to predominance given to consumer culture and entertainment by global television channels, which in many cases has taken bad shape in the present scenario.

In recent year, Indian audiences have been exposed to international programme contents and this led to shift in viewing patterns. Now entertainment hold the prime position.

All these are happening despite content regulation by the Ministry of I & B, which bans any material offensive to good taste or decency or threatens the integrity of the nation by encouraging violence or antinational attitude or which contains visuals or words that reflect a slandering ironical and snobbish attitude to the portrayal of certain ethnic, linguistic and regional groups. Besides this, material which encourages superstitious belief, or denigration of women and children is also banned. Broadcasting Bill (1997) also speaks about regulation of television content carried by licensed services. There is no specific regulatory limits on the level of foreign programming as the nature of audience demand largely determines that the bulk of content to be produced in India. This Bill also provides a range of guidelines including:-

(a) Compensation for the declining scope of content regulation to ensure that all society's communication needs are met;

(b) to counter-act the danger of media concentration in the private sector; and

(c) to counter-act any shortfalls of commercial television in respect of providing quality News and public informations.

The existing code though mandatory is too vague to be effective. It only speaks about the action against a channel and cable operator in case of indecent portrayal of women. To strengthen the regulatory authority, in October 2005, the Ministry of I&B, constituted a committee headed by S.C. Arora, I&B Secretary to revise television advertisement and programming codes. The exercise is a prelude to the constitution of a television content regulatory authority, likely to be set up by mid'2006. This new code will be more comprehensive and also cover new trends including News channels. The necessity for a comprehensive and new code for content reveals that with the globalization of Indian broadcasting, the control of government on global television has become weak and especially in the case of those countries were mushroom growth of TV dish antenna has taken place due to its open sky policy, which is mentioned below:

Table: 5.3
Private Dish Ownership

Unrestricted	Permitted	Restricted
Australia	Bangladesh	China
Hongkong	India	Malaysia
Korea	Myanmar	Singapore
Taiwan	Philippines	

(Source: Asia-Pacific Broadcasting, February' 1994)

One of the direct result of permission to set up dish antenna by private players has resulted in the drop in the viewership of Doordarshan programmes. Its popular programmes such as Mahabharata crossed 90.0 percent television viewership rating before advent of the global TV. Today, the rating of the most popular programme i.e; 'Hindi Film' is down by 49.0 percent and the most popular serial of few years back, i.e., 'Jungle Book' rating came down to 36.0 per cent (Karnik, 1993). This trend continue in recent years also.

Another outcome of the goverment liberalization policy in case of Indian Broadcasting i.e.; opening of the Indian sky through dish/satellite medium has also increased the global flow of television programmes, mostly from the western countries. As the local programme production capacities cannot keep pace with the expansion of television timing which further resulted in the import of foreign programmes usually from the industrialized countries, particularly from USA, which is given below.

Tabel: 5.4
Percentage of US Programming

Site	1962	1972	1982	1992
Japan	7	9	4	5
South Korea	24	19	10	9
Hong Kong	69	28	9	2
Taiwan	36	21	9	20
India	N/A	3	0	0
France	0	3	6	22
Spain	13	24	11	31
Sweden	8	2	4	34
Israel	N/A	13	15	15
Lebanon	24	41	34	29
Dominican Republic	14	22	36	N/A

Contd...

Site	1962	1972	1982	1992
Colombia	18	10	23	N/A
Chile	4	38	28	22
Brazil	31	44	37	20
Mexico	38	26	35	24
Anglo-Canada	49	50	53	51
Franco-Canada	35	38	38	39
Trinidad	29	50	59	69
Jamaica	30	46	55	65
Barbados	31	31	52	N/A

Source: Adapted from Straubhaar 2001:148

Keeping in view the global flow of television programmes, some of the early studies on globalization of broadcasting were done to investigate this aspect. These studies concentrated on the supply of foreign programmes fare in national broadcast. For instance, the studies analysed the proportion of imported material in the output of national channels and the countries from which such material was imported. It was also assumed in the early study that if there was supply, there would be consumption with generally negative effects as a result of the adoption of foreign values and life styles. For example during 1980s there were concerns raised about the Dallasisation of media culture across the world as a result of availability of US soaps such as Dallas to diverse audience. With the globalization of the US model of television, such American programmes, as 'Baywatch', 'Friends', 'ER' and 'The Simpsons' have a global viewership, although in media rich countries like India, they remain very marginal or negligable to the mainstream media consumption as can be seen from the above table in which in 1992, the percentage of US programming was nil for India although the advent of global satellite television has already taken place. After 1992 some US programming came through global television in India. The flow of the television programmes in other direction is a mere trickle by comparison (McBride, 1980) which is based on the assumption that international television flow among countries have cultural and economic effects in a specific regions or on specific groups of viewers (i.e., Media Imperialism). But it is not out of context to mention here that audience response to global programming are highly differentiated depending in part on the level of exposure to national, regional and global fare and in part on the social characteristics of specific public. Availability of cultural fare even if it is widely watched doesnot necessarily imply that its values and ideological contents are accepted uncritically. On the other hand, provided that cultural imports are widely consumed audience resistance has little significance for media conglomerates in charge of programming.

Supply of foreign programmes materials is only one level in the process of acculturation of global media. There are other steps as show below:

Table : 5.5

Level of Transnational flow of television material

Independent Variable	Dependent Variable
a) Independent flow of television programmes	Transnationalization of television supply
b) Transnationalization of total supply	Transnationalization of Consumption
c) Transnationalization of total consumption	Potential cultural effects

It recognizes that while supply of material is a pre-condition for the consumption of such matrial, these have to be treated at two different variables in order to understand the cultural effects on the recipient countries.

(A) Some Study Report on TV Programme Supply and Consumption:-

(1) In 1990, AMIC with assistance from UNESCO launched a study on television programme, supply and consumption in four Asia-Pacific countries, namely, Australia, India, Philippines and Republic of Korea. The study examined foreign programmes in national broadcast and bilateral spill over of national broadcast to neighbouring countries. It took sample data for a period of two week. Table given below show the share of imported programmes in total national television programme supply by programme category for the above mentioned four countries.

It is clear from the table given below that the supply of foreign progammes vary greatly from country to country. In Australia, it comprised 54.2 per cent whereas in India, it was 8.3 percent. In India, sports programme appear to comprise the bulk of foreign programme (4.5%). However, it can be said that at the time of the selection of Indian sample international test cricket matches were being played by the Indians and this perhaps account for the dominance of sports programmes in the sample.

In term of consumption, Drama/Movies appear to be the most popular general programme. In India, it was only 2.6 percent in comprasion to other

Table: 5.6 : Share of Imported Programmes in Total National Television Programme Supply by Programme Category

Programme Category	Australia M*	Australia %	India M	India %	Philippines M	Philippines %	Korea M	Korea %
1. Drama/movies	2167..7	36.2	20.2	2.6	688.9	14.4	171.8	4.6
2. Light entertainment	434.8	7.3	0.0	0.0	404.3	8.4	71.0	1.9
3. Music	29.2	0.5	0.0	0.0	84.0	1.8	0.0	0.0
4. Sports	113.6	1.9	35.7	4.5	21.8	0.4	5.0	0.1
5. News	178.5	3.0	0.0	0.0	31.1	0.6	20.1	0.5
6. Information	0.0	0.0	2.0	0.3	158.6	3.3	8.0	0.2
7. Arts	22.7	0.4	0.0	0.0	46.6	0.9	59.0	1.6
8. Education	292.0	4.9	7.1	0.9	9.3	0.2	0.0	0.0
9. Religious	0.0	0.0	0.0	0.0	116.6	2.4	0.0	0.0
10. Others	0.0	0.0	0.0	0.0	0.0	0.0	0.0	0.0
Total	**3245.0**	**54.2**	**65.0**	**8.3**	**1555.0**	**32.7**	**335.0**	**8.9**

M* = minutes

Source: Sepstrup and Goonesekera (1994), TV Transnationalization : Europe and Asia

countries under study where it was higher. However, the situation in India has changed since 1992 when STAR TV became freely available. In September, 1992, it was estimated that STAR TV had penetrated 3.7 percent of total households on an all India basis; 5.0 percent in urban areas and 10.0 percent to 20.0 percent in major cities (Karnik, 1993). Obviously the potential for exposure of Indians to foreign programmes is now very much greater than when this study was done in 1991.

(2) Another study conducted by UNESCO in 1994 also reveals that in India the young and the educated viewers living in metropolitan were heavier consumer than others and women were likely to watch more television programmes than men. There were only few foreign programmes and exposure to it was comparatively higher among men than women, the young than the elderly and metropolitan rather than rural people. Of the total foreign programmes viewed, three quarter of these were sports programme. The choices for these programmes can easily be explained in term of the extent to which women and men are able to identify with various types of media content. As women mostly prefer serials, soap operas and telenovelas, whereas men prefer for sports, News and other current affair programmes. Most probably this is in their psyche.

Table given below indicate the co-efficient of utilization of programmes provided by national television. The objective of this table is to explore the total programme percentage available to a viewer actually viewed by him or her.

Table: 5.7
Coefficients of utilization of national programming supply

	Australia	India	Philippines	Korea
Origin	%	%	%	%
Domestic	4.4	12.0	1.9	3.9
Foreign	2.1	3.1	2.6	5.4
Total supply	**3.2**	**11.3**	**2.2**	**4.0**

Source: Sepstrup and Goonesekera (1994), TV Transnationalization: Europe and Asia

It is clear from the above table that in India 12.0 percent of domestic and 3.1 percent of the foreign programme broadcasting times were actually consumed by the viewers. Hence, there is a scope of great competition to attract audiences. In case of Korea and Philippines, there is a higher percentage of use of foreign programmes than of domestic ones. Except few countries in Asia, the utilization of foreign programming supply is greater and in most cases USA dominate the content of programmes imposing indirectly their culture, values and ideologies on the recipient countries. In India also many long running American soap operas/cartoons have been dubbed in hindi to make them more attractive without changing its content. However dubbed cartoons are more popular which are telecast on different satellite channels, such as, Zee, STAR Plus, Sony, Disney, Cartoon Network etc. Some of these are 'Teenage Mutant Ninja 'Turtle', G.I. Joe, Batman, Spiderman, He-man, Superman, Alladin, Flash Gordon, Defenders of the Earth and Duck Tales etc; out of series of Cartoon shows.

(B) Study on Content Analysis of some satellite channels including Doordarshan

The content analysis of seven Hindi television channels, two from Doordarshan and five from private channels, sampled during the month of August and September, 1997 reveals the following facts.

The dominant content among them is Hindi Films with EL TV screening the highest number of films followed by Sony TV and then by other channels. Films have been followed by film based programmes on every channel, the most popular being song sequences from film sponsored by a number of commercial companies as part of their advertising strategy. These channels, mostly shows some kind of half an hour serialized drama (soap operas) or serials. The story lines of these serials are based on contemporary social issues and relationships, religious and Mythological stories or the saga of some historical personality. No television channel can afford to do without broadcast of regular serial. Zee TV tops the list in Hindi serials followed by STAR Plus which provides both Hindi and English serials (except Doordarshan channels). These are given below in tabular form:

Except for Sony and EL TV, all channels have news on weekdays. Doordarshan, Zee television telecast news seven days a week. While Doordarshan and Star Plus have news in Hindi and English language, for other channels the News is in 'Hinglish'.

Table: 5.8 Content Distribution of Programmes in Selected Seven Television Channels per Week*

Broad Programme Content	Name of the Channel							
	Door-darshan-1	Door-darshan-2	El TV	Home TV	Sony	Star Plus	Zee TV	Total
Contemporary, historical and mythological drama and serials	45	71	18	22	24	38	39	257
Movies and film based programmes	10	11	46	6	22	12	10	117
Art, culture, classical dance and music, religious discourse and region specific programmes	13	10	1	4	2	13	12	55
News, political and current affairs	5	9	-	3	-	5	4	26
Education, Social and environment	8	7	2	-	-	3	5	25
Uncategorised and other programmes	28	12	4	11	1	8	4	68
Total	**109**	**120**	**71**	**46**	**49**	**79**	**74**	**548**

*Frequency has been counted in terms of the number of programmes in each category regardless of duration, excluding all commecials and development or social messages.

Table: 5.9

Distribution of Time Devoted to Public Sphere per Week in Selected Seven Television Channels*

Name of the Channel	Time Davoted to Public-Sphere (in minutes)	Time Devoted to Recreation and Entertainment (in minutes)	Total Telecast Time (in minutes)
Doordarshan 1	1,564 (19.6)	6,416 (80.4)	7,980 (100.0)
Doordarshan 2	1,185 (16.6)	5,955 (83.4)	7,140 (100.0)
EL TV	210 (2.1)	9,870 (97.9)	10,080 (100.0)
Home TV	510 (7.5)	5,916 (92.5)	6,426 (100.0)
Sony	0 (0.0)	10,080 (100.0)	10,080 (100.0)
Star Plus	1,005 (10.0)	9,075 (90.0)	10,080 (100.0)
Zee TV	945 (9.4)	9,135 (90.6)	10,080 (100.0)
Total	**5,419 (8.8)**	**56,447 (91.2)**	**61,866 (100.0)**

* While five channels telecast 24 hours of programming, Doordarshan 1 and 2 together telecast for 16 hours per day (Now 24 hrs.)

From the above table, it is clear that time devoted to public sphere is much more on Doordarshan channels than other satellite channels. It includes social marketing, public concerns on major issues such as pollution, population, politics, national integration and other social and legal issues.

Content Trends

The report prepared by CII-KPMG titled "Indian entertainment industry focus 2010: Dreams to Reality", speaks about the future of the television content in context of India which is currently estimated at Rs. 28.0 billion software industry. The study further speaks about the increased number of programmes on prime time and enhanced audience interest in niche content due to globalization in this field. While mainstream entertainment programming will continue to be the bulk of Indian television, other genres such as News, sports, children and special interests (i.e, religion, home, health etc.) will form an increasingly important part of the software pie. The report further speak about boom in television sector and the spiralling demand for content but television houses are unable to cope up with growing demand of TV contents except few who have consolidated their position in this field. Going forward, it is believed that both broadcasters and content producers will begin to work out backward and forward integration models respectively with broadcasters developing a higher proportion of content in–house and more production houses getting into the broadcasting business.

Another growth area in the Indian television software industry will be adaptation of the existing content for digital and on other delivery platforms. Most of the Indian television software is generated on analog platform, going digital only in the last phase of broadcasting. So all the contents need to be converted in required format to suit the technological development in this field.

As in many other countries, globalization in relation to India has profoundly influenced its media cultures, forcing it to redefine its place in the world. However this influence has been a two way process. India has absorbed and adapted aspects of global modernity but a lot from India - popular music, film, fashion, literature - has also been globalized in the 1990s as a result of marketization. In the 21st century, television from India is likely to become part of global television culture - after all every Sixth person in the world is of South Asian Origin.

References

- Expert Committee Report: An Indian Personality for Television' (Vol. 1), March 1985, I & B Ministry, N. Delhi.
- Agrawal, Binod C. "The Meaning of Hinglishness: Liberalization and Globalization in Indian Broadcasting", in Cultural and Political Responsibilities (ed) Kevin Robins, United Nations World Television Forum.
- Artzy, Lee (Spring, 2005), "Paradigm Shudders" in Global Media Journal, Vol. 4, Issue-6, Purdue University, Calumet.
- Boyd-Barret O and Newbold, C (eds) "Approaches to Media; A Reader (1995), Tunbridge wells, Gray Publishing.
- Boyd-Barret O, "(1988)", Media Imperialism, Reformalated Electronic Empires: Global Media and Local Resistance, Arnold, London.
- Banerjee, I. "(2002), Media Globalization and Localization in the New Asian TV Landscape', in Gazette: The International Journal for Communication Studies.
- Baker, C. (1999) "Television, Globalization and Cultural Identities, Open University Press, Buckingham, London.
- Crane, Diana "Cultural Globalization from the Perspective of the Sociology of Culture, University of Pennsylvania, USA.
- Eashwar S. Sucharita (ed.) Oct. 2003, "Response to Globalization and the Digital Divide in the Asia-Pacific", Asia-Pacific Institute of Broadcasting Development, Singapore.
- Ferguson, M. (1995), "Media Market and Identities: Reflections on the Global-Local Dialectic", University of Marlyland, US, in Canadian Journal of Communication, vol. 20, No.4.
- Goonasekera, Anura" Global Satellite Broadcasting Service: Educational & Cultural Contribution in UNESCO report on Cultural and Educational Dimension, Asian Mass Communication Research Centre, Singapore.

- Indian Entertainment-Industry Focus 2010: Dreams to Reality - A CII-KPMG Report (Page: 23-44)
- Joshi S.R. (1998) " Transporder Television in India" in Goonasekera, A & Lee P (eds.)" TV without Borders: Asia Speaks Out", Asian Média Information and Communication Centre, Singapore.
- Joshi. S.R. & Trivedi, Bela (1994). "Mass Media and Cross Cultural Communication: A Study of Television in India", Development and Communication Unit, ISRO, Ahmedabad.
- Kumar, Kewal J. (1981), "Mass Communication in India", Jaico Publication, Delhi.
- Karnik, K.S. (1993), "Socio-Cultural and Economic Impact of Transnational Broadcasting and Cable TV.", Publication of the International Broadcasting, Cable & Satellite Conference, N.Delhi.
- Mcchesney, Robert W. "(March 2001)," Global Media, Neoliberalism and Imperialism in Monthly Review, Vol. 52, No. 10.
- Mukherjee, Arpita (Oct, 2004)". Trade and Culture" (Draft Paper), UNESCO.
- Modoux, Alain (Gen. Ed.)" 1997, World Communication Report: The Media & the Challenge of New Technologies, UNESCO, chapter on "Media Globalization and Regulation."
- MacBride, Sean (1980) "Many Voices, One World", UNESCO, Paris.
- Mohammadi, A Sreberny Winseek, D. McKenna, J & Boyd Barett O. (eds.) 1997, "Media in Global Context: A Reader, Arnold. London.
- Pathania, Geetika "Responses to Transnational TV in a STAR Stuck land: DD & Star TV in India in Melkote, S R Shields, Agarwal B.C. (eds.) "International Satellite Broadcasting in Asia, University Press of America, Marlyland.

- (Dr.) Postill, John (April 2005), "Media Anthropology in a World of States (Draft Report), Bik, University of Bremen.
- Page, David & Crawley, William (2001), "Satellite Over South Asia: Broadcasting and the Public Interest", " Sage, Delhi/London.
- Rai, Vivek "Media Studies Conference-2002, paper on Media and Globalization".
- Sepstrup, P. & Goonasekera, A., (1994) "TV Transnationalization: Europe and Asia, UNESCO, Paris.
- Straubhaar, J. (2003), "Choosing National TV: Cultural, Capital, Language and Cultural Proximity in Brazil in Elasmar, M. (ed.) "The Impact of International TV, A Paradigm Shift". LEA Publishers, London.
- Sinclair, John and Harrison, Mark "Globalization and Television in Asia: The case of India and China, Victoria University of Technology, Australia
- TRAI Report, (GOI) New Delhi.
- Television Asia, December' 2003.
- Thussu, D.K. "Taming the Dragon and The Elephant: Murdoch's Media in Asia". (Paper)
- (Dr.) Ulla, Carlsson "The Rise and Fall of NWICO and Then", NORDICOM, Goteborg University, Box 713, SE 40530, Goteberg.

6

Epilogue

The global television has not only become a part but also a central agent of the capitalist system. This type of television promote a corporate agenda in its different activities. Now, it has become a deterritorialized medium also since it no longer confined to the national boundaries. At the same time it has territorializing effect. As in many other countries, globalization in relation to India has profoundly influenced its media culture forcing it to redefine its place in the world. However, this influence has been a two way process. In context of India, it has absorbed and adapted aspects of global modernity and also a lot from India- popular music, films, fashion, literature etc. - has been globalized in the 1990s as a result of marketization. In the 21st century, television from India is likely to become a part of global television culture – after all every 6th person on the globe is of south Asian origin. To understand the changes that has occured in the last few decades, the commercialization, and deregulation of national television system has to be kept in mind, which began worldwide in the 1970s and 1980s and reached its full speed in the 1990s (Herman & McChensey, 1997).

Broadly, we can categorise different aspects of global television in the following way:-

(i) There has been a several fold increase in the number of television channels in the country due to the forces of liberalization and commercialization,

(ii) There has been alteration of the programming or media content to suit the corporate interest; and

(iii) There has been an exponential rise in advertising expenditure in India due to globalization of television. All the above aspects have been discussed in the ensuing pargraphs:-

The rise of cable and satellite technology has opened up national market to scores of new channels. The primary providers of these channels are the media transnational companies that dominate cable television channel ownership and have aggressively established numerous global editions of their channels. (e.g.: STAR, Sony, ZEE TV etc.) to accomodate new market in different continents. These transnationals operates in joint venture to serve their own interest, (e.g. STAR with TATA with regard to the DTH system). This has influenced media culture forcing it to redefine such venture in global world. If we look at the rise of these cable and satellite channels in the past fifteen years, we will come across many of the development that has taken place in the world, such as, the development of television markets technological innovations, convergence processes in telecommunication, and a crisis that occured in many public television system. All these factors have contributed in bringing changes in the television scenario. Here, it is pertinent to discuss the most important factor, i.e., crisis in the public television system which gave boost to the development and rise of global television system:-

(a) Reduction in the growth rate of revenue from licence fees to lower level than the increase in costs in many countries;

(b) The number of channels has increased exponentially due to the segmentation of supply and the globalization of some niche markets (e.g.; News and Music) enormously enlarging the choice available to the viewing public;

(c) Globalization of information industries have progressively broken down the boundaries between traditionally separate industries such as television; and

(d) Marginalization in viewership and advertising.

Doordarshan, had a monopoly till 1991 and without any competition in this field, the whole of the advertising revenue of television reached to it. After 1991, with the advent of cable and satellite television channels like STAR, CNN, Sony, ZEE TV; etc. the position of Doordarshan was shaken and the advertising revenue began to fall for DD. Besides this, it has some negative impacts on the quality and content of Doordarshan due to competition from other Cable & Satellite channels.

The process of liberalizing the television markets and the entry of new operators and new services have aggravated the problems of the public broadcasting. From the economic point of view the most important problems arising from the simultaneous presence of subsidised public operators on the same market are the possible distortion in competitiveness in different aspects for these global television.

As stated, the convergence and conglomeration of existing commercial media also opened up new markets for media giants in a sense that we live in a 'New Information Order' of market freedom controlled by a handful of corporations. This liberalization and commercialization has taken place at the expense of the previously dominant State-run system (e.g. in case of India: Doordarshan, Herman & Mcchensey 1997). Countries which had in place State run public service television were forced to accept competition from transnational media on their previously national air waves (Supreme Court of India order on airwaves control; all C&S channels are free to use). The outlook for many of the public service broadcasters look dismal despite having a larger chunk of audiences on their part, but now it is declining world wide due to comparison by their audience to the timely and well defined programming and content of global commercial services, and renaissance of ethnic subcultures by these global channels, often located geographically across borders (e.g. television in Indian languages have found audiences in Bangladesh, Srilanka, Malaysia, Gulf States, Fiji, Mauritius and other countries). This have its echos in the UNESCO and now it has also shifted to WTO. Overall the commitment of these global television is to encourage the establishment of commercial media globally to better serve the need of a market economy.

Because the media conglomerates are commercially run, their content must be profitable.

This has led to the increased infotainment on global tv as well as of the global audience, while the educational role, the television used to play has been either left behind and forgotten or ignored. The commodification of content necessarily carries with it an ideological baggage as the ideas put forward are those linked with consumption (in advertising) and the opening of market (in News programming). Issues of major concern to the developing countries are almost absent from global television News (Thussu, 1998), instead of this, it has created a new category of global events such as Olympic Games, world Cup, Tiananmen square, Gulf wars, Princess Diana's Death and funeral and so on which suits their interest. Besides this, globalized television has glocalized their programmes, which can be seen in their soap operas and other relatively low budget contents. In many cases, Indianization of American formats has taken place which in turn has created a new model of hybridization between the East and the West. Today, we proudly have our own clones of the global programmes (e.g. Who Wants to Be a Millionaire', CATS, Road Rules, The weakest link, Deal or No Deal, American Idol etc.,). Some of our television sitcoms, programme formats and the presentation styles look as if they have been produced by the same studios. Various countries do it in their own languages having different faces and India also falls under this category. By rebroad-casting and reversioning of imported global contents, our own media have been reinforcing it in a subliminal way the global cultural which have become common currency today in many countries. Perhaps, this may be the real impact of globalization on our television. One major outcome of this media marriage is the development of 'Hinglish' - a mixture of English, the language of international media and Hindi, the most widely used language in India. In this process to some extent, it has lost its diversity and ability to present different points of view.

Media conglomerates encourages popular tastes to become more uniform, which has led to homogeneity of programme content. Gerbner (1982) called it 'Mainstreaming'. This may be due to concentration of both delivery system and content of global information network by media conglomerates. Media critiques view it as 'Cultural Imperialism' -- control by developed countries on delivery system, content and information system. But in the present situation it is not true. Now-a-days, the third world countries are producing and exporting content developed in their own countries (e.g. Mexico, India, China, etc.) which is very much popular among global audiences. So, we have to understand this phenomenon in term of transnational corporate cultural domination. Media Advocacy Group critiquing the homogenous content of the multi channel universe are raising serious concerns about the ability of a market driven media culture to represent the milieu of the complex social classes that constitute India. As far as News and Sports programmes are concerned, audiences liked global television in India. As regard to other foreign programmes, the Indian audiences prefer having programmes with Indian culture and values like Drama, Serials, and Plays. Indian audiences do watch foreign programmes, but some of them are having harmful effect on them (e.g programmes related to sex, violence and crime). But these are having short term effect on audience. The main impact of these programmes, which have long impact are their consumerist, instant - gratification and even hedonistic undertone. Most of these are antithetical to traditional Indian social values and are directed to satisfy the needs of advertisers and the affluent audiences to which advertisers are attracted. This has led to the exclusion of the majority of Indians – the poor especially those living in the country side from the purview of their programming.

Regarding content, Jean-Gabrial Manguy of Radio, Australia has provided some possible solutions, which are as follows:-

(a) In order to control content homogenization and to avoid cultural uniformity, we urgently need diversity that means access to wider range of content. For this 'Right Free Agreement' among Asia-Pacific countries to facilitate reciprocal access to content on a non-commercial basis be implemented. The Asian Broadcasting Union has already gone some distance down the path with its web-based programme exchange and the daily Asia News service.

(b) The exchange of more content must not only be done just on television or in English, but on other medium and in other regional languages too. A number of organisations already distribute their content across the region via satellite. A daily bouquet of Hindi programme and others could be made available to all broadcaster who are interested in rebroadcasting, and

(c) Concerned persons should be encouraged to generate more content of local relevance keeping in view our rich cultural heritage to tide the wave of globalization.

For the maximisation of market share, trans-national corporations are using the advantage of scale of economy and financial power to create a world of instantaneous and depthless communication, which is in no way related to the enhancement of public life or culture of the third world countries. It is a way for global television to link itself with the market economy. And in this connection advertising on global television has helped these TNCs to develop a whole new market in South Asia including India, both for new products and a whole new range of consumers goods. Besides targeting the Indian market, it has also created audiences across the borders for its products. The proliferation of corporate advertising and commercial entertainment has flooded the Indian market in recent years, by providing images of different life styles and gender.

Vilanilam (1989) , in this context, has observed that television advertising in India presents a heterogenous cross-section of the Indian populance with the images of products and lifestyle that are economically out of reach for the vast majority. In this way, advertising constitutes an imaginary world of desire that address not only to the elites that can purchase such goods and in doing so affirm their elite status. But the masses of Indians are poor for whom the imaginaire is merely a reference point, a shaper of aspirations, an ideal model of success, pleasure and envy.

Global television propagates global consumer culture that is wasteful, unjust and environmentally unsound. And when this culture is put forward as the only one to aspire for, it perpetuates economic disparities and unsustainable life style. This situation has also created condition for social tension by undermining culture and by promoting consumerism. It replaces reality and what ever falls beyond the penumbra of the home screen. According to Kiran

Karnik MD, Discovery communication in India, Commercialism completely overtook the professed developmental communication objectives. In this regard, Stephen Barnard has pointed out that commercialization of mass media is that pursuit of advertising revenue which marginalizes less popular tastes and interest. It creates an environment most conducive to reception of advertising message leading to programming that is undermining, unchallanging and pacifying.

Globalization of television has given a fillip to Indian entreprenuers to promote their media interest in India. The global spread of media is here to stay. So we have to learn to live with it and in order to harness its potential for good, one should look at it as an opportunity to open one's eyes through education and experiences and not to close them in fear and ignorance and for this certain measures have to be adopted, which are as follows:-

(i) We have to encourage cultural and educational functions of satellite broadcasting;

(ii) Serious consideration must be given to the formulation of an agreed code of ethics -- a minimum set of Acts and guidelines - which satellite broadcasting must adhere to, for smooth relationship with government, audience and the channel providers. (e.g.; The (Indian) cable Act 1994, which tries to regulate the TV broadcasting scene in India. This law clearly applies to transnational TV broadcast when such broadcasts are retelecast through Indian Cable companies. ICA stipulates that no programme or advertisement can be transmitted in India unless it is in conformity with prescribed programme and advertising code. Unless, the problem like Gandhi gaffe in 'Nikki tonight' programme broadcast in India by STAR TV will happen. For this the Indian Parliament accused Murdoch of cultural terrorism. The Asian Broadcasting Union in 1994 in Kyoto, Japan, adopted certain guidelines, which places emphasis on respecting the cultural diversity in the Asia-Pacific region rather than on creating a common transnational culture in this region that should be observed in toto. In line of this, there is also guidelines on the programme contents of global satellite television broadcasting in this region.)

(iii) National television channels (e.g.; Doordarshan and its regional variants) must improve their own programmes to make them more attractive, especially for the young and women audience. For this restructuring and refocussing Doordarshan must be a priority despite the concern that it can, perhaps, deliver the public goods in proper manner and ways; and

(iv) A marketing scheme for cultural product from different countries should be encouraged. The main idea is to make the availability of programmes from a variety of sources known to the broadcasters.

It has also been proposed that media ownership be restricted to holding a licence for a particular broadcasting distribution (e.g., satellite broadcaster couldnot be licenced to provide cable services). Also ownership in any category could not hold more than 20.0 percent stake in any other broadcasting company. Now the PM- empowered ICE Committee has given some radical suggestions to provide a new direction on convergence, which is helpful for smooth and healthy development of global television in India. Some of these are:-

Barriers to entry in cable television should be removed through policy intervention and guidelines put in place for facilitating/ securing right-of-way permissions.

There should be no pre-censorship for television. A suitable self-regulatory mechanism for all content may be considered. An over-arching content regulator may oversee such arrangements.

Link licensing for television channels to a single-window clearance system with the Ministry of Information and Broadcasting, and consider setting timeframes and norms of transparency.

References

- Appadurai, A (1996) "Modernity At Large: Cultural Dimensions of Globalization": University of Minnesota Press, Minneapolis.
- Dixit, Kunda, "Star Wars: Conflicts and Media in the Satellite Age". (Paper).
- David, Page & William Crawley (2001), "Satellite Over South Asia; Broadcasting and the Public Interest", Sage Publication, N. Delhi.
- Desai, Mira Kapil, "Monographic: Indian Television in the Era of Globalization: Unity, Diversity or Disparity?", SNDT Women University, Mumbai, India.
- Global Media Journal (2005), Vol. 4, Issue - 7, "Public Service Broadcasting: A Best Practices Source Book, AMIC & UNESCO.
- Goonasekera, Anura, "Global Satellite Broadcasting Service: Educational & Cultural Contributions", Asian Mass Communication Research & Information Centre, Singapore, (Cultural & Educational Dimensions, UNESCO, Paris, C-II, 96/WS/8).
- " " (1993) "Media Technology and Social Imperatives: An Examination of Communication Policies in Selected Asian Countries," Media Asia, Vol-20, No.4, AMIC, Singapore.

- Gupta, Nilanjana (1998) 'Switchning Channels: Ideologies of Television in India', Oxford University Press, Delhi.
- Griffin, M. (2002) "From Cultural Imperialism to Transnational Commercialization: Shifting Paradigms......", Global Media Journal, Vol–1.
- Hindustan Times, " ICE task force not on convergence", February 20, 2006.
- Herman, E & McChesney, R. (1997) The Global Media: The New Missionaries of Global Capitalism", Casell, Washington DC.
- Khushu, O.P. (1993) "Satellite Communication in Asia: An Overview", Media Asia, Singapore.
- Kumar, Keval, J. (1997) "Mass Communication in India", Jaico Publishing House, Bombay.
- Kumar, Aashish (1999), "Localizing the Global India: New Imperatives for International Communication Scholarship in the Satellite Era", TBS, Adham Centre for TV Journalism, American University, Cairo.
- Poorananda, Dasegowdanakoplu," Expanding Media Market & Shrinking Public Sphere", (Paper), Mangalore University. Web: WWW.Jhu-edu ....
- Pavarala, Vinod & Kumar, Kanchan (2001), "Legislating for Community Radio Policy Framework for Other Countries in Voices for Change", A Journal on Communication for Development, Vol.5, No.1.
- Rohit & Vikas, R.M. "Media, Rising consumer Culture and the Working Class", (Paper) IIT, Kanpur.
- Robert, W. McChesney (2001), "Global Media, Neoliberalism and Imperialism", Monthly Review, Vol. 52, No.-10.
- Tracey, M. (1993) "The Decline and Fall of Public Services", Oxford University press, Delhi.
- Thussu, D.K. (1998) "Introduction in Electronic Empires: Global Media and Local Resistance", Arnold, London.
- UNESCO Handbook on Public Service Broadcasting.
- Werner, Vom. Busch (ed.) 2004, "The Asian Media Directory", Konard-Adenauer Foundation, Singapore.

Appendices

N0.4/58/2000-PC
Government of India
Ministry of Information & Broadcasting

New Delhi Dated 16.7.2001

OFFICE MEMORANDUM

In pursuance of Planning Commission's O.M. No. 4(4)/35/2000-C&I dated 23.4.2001 constituting Working Group on I&B sector for the Tenth Five year Plan, it has been decided to set up the following sub-groups :

1. **Sub-group on 'Content Creation and Software'**

i) Shri Mark Tully

ii) Shri Kiran Karnik

iii) Shri Ram Gopal Bajaj

iv) Shri Bhuvan Lall

v) Shri M.K. Ghosh, Dir(I), Planning Commission

vi) Shri Sudhir Sharma, JS(P)

vii) Smt A.C.Duggal, JS(F)

viii) Shri Rakesh Mohan, JS(B) ... **Convenor**

2. Sub-group on 'Carriage and Technology'

i) Shri Anil Baijal, AS(B)/CEO:PB

ii) Shri Buvan Lall,

iii) Shri Kiran Karnik

iv) Shri K.R.P. Verma, Director(BECIL)

v) Prof. S.Raghava Chari, IIMC

vi) Shri R.N Choubey, Director, Min. of Finance

vii) Shri R.C.Mishra, E.D:PB .... **Convenor**

3. Sub-group on 'Human Resourcement Development'

i) Dr. Mohan Agashe, Director, FTII

ii) Shri Ram Gopal Bajaj, Director, NSD

iii) Shri Sandeep Bedi,

iv) Representative of Ministry of HRD

v) Smt A.C.Duggal, JS(F)

vi) Shri Sudhir Sharma, JS(P) ... **.Convenor**

4. Sub-group on 'Traditional Media Unit'

i) Shri Mark Tully

ii) Shri Ram Gopal Bajaj, Director, NSD

iii) Smt A.C. Duggal, JS(F)

iv) Shri Sudhir Sharma, JS(P) **....Convenor**

2. The respective Working Groups will go into details in the concerned areas and make

assessment of the future requirements and submit recommendations/suggestions for consideration of the Working Group, within the terms of reference.

3. The sub-group on HRD will examine the nature and extent of Government's involvement required in Films Sector. Documentary Films & Films Division would be covered by the sub-group on "Content Creation & Software".

4. The sub-groups shall submit their preliminary report by 25.7.2001 and final report by 15.8.2001 positively.

(SUDIR SHARMA)
Joint Secretary &
Convenor, Working Group

Copy to :

1. Shri Anil Baijal, AS (B) & CEO:PB
2. Smt Aruna Makhan, AS & FA
3. Shri Sudhir Sharma, JS(P)
4. Shri Rakesh Mohan, JS(B)
5. Smt A.C.Duggal., JS(F)
6. Shri R.C. Mishra, ED:PB
7. Shri K.S.Sarma, Ministry of HRD : It is requested that the name & address of the representative from Ministry of HRD for sub-group on "Human Resourcement Development" may kindly be intimated.
8. All other Members of the sub-groups

(SUDIR SHARMA)
Joint Secretary &
Convenor, Working Group

Copy to Sr. PPS to Secretary(I&B)

Appendix-1

Commercial Rate card with guidelines for DD programmes:

I. SPONSORED PROGRAMMES

(a)

(i) Booking is acceptable either of a client or of a product/ service. In case of a product, Free Commercial Time (FCT) can be utilised for the advertisements of that product / service only.

(ii) The Sponsor (s) / Client (s) is allowed to advertise any number of products in the admissible commercial time.

(iii) Commercial Breaks permitted in all programmes are:

a. Three commercial breaks in a 30 minute slot, four commercial breaks in a 45 minute slot and six commercial breaks in a 60 minute slot will be allowed.

b. In case of sponsored programmes produced by outsiders, the Free Commercial Time (FCT) will be inserted by producer.

c. DD will retain right to use upto 60 seconds in-between the programme with every 30 minute slot and 120 seconds in every 60 minute slot for advertisements, channel promotion, public service messages. For this, a break bumper is to be provided by the producer at mid-break for insertion of the material from Doordarshan end.

(iv) Advertisements featuring the artists participating in a particular serial / programme are also accepted for telecast alongwith the same programme.

(b) Credit Lines

In addition to Free Commercial Time, the sponsor (s) are allowed credit lines, upto 20 seconds at the beginning and upto 20 seconds at the end of the programme in case of programmes on Channel -1 / Channel -2 / Regional channels and Regional Kendras. In case of continuing programme (e.g. feature film, sports etc.) with different sponsors in each 30 minute slots, the credit lines for 20 seconds each will be supered over the programme in such a manner that it does not obstruct the viewing of the programme.

The telecast of the credit lines will be governed as follows :-

(1) Programme Sponsored in the Name of the Client (Company) : The credit lines may contain :

a. Visual presentation of the name of the company in any lettering / style choice and / or name in audio (including accompanying music, if desired).

b. Visual presentation of the standard logo of the company, if desired, and,

c. Any colour scheme of the company for visual presentation, and if so with special effects.

(2) Programme Sponsored in the name of a product:

The credit lines may contain the name of the product, spoken or written on any style, with or without accompanying music. Display of products with punchline is allowed. The duration of the sponsor / punchline can go upto a maximum of 5 seconds.

II. NUMBER OF SPONSORS ALLOWED

1. There shall be no limit to the number of sponsors for a programme.
2. The sponsor tag should be on the punchline of the product. However its duration should not exceed a total of 5 seconds.

III. BANKING

100% continuous banking shall be allowed in all programmes till the end of the programme. Each single episode shall not carry commercials more than admissible FCT + 60 seconds of banked FCT (per half an hour). No cross programme / cross channel banking shall be allowed. Banking to lapse with the end of programme. Banking of 30 seconds allowed to sponsored programme on DD-India which they get on DD-I non-prime time is discontinued with immediate effect. However, if any programme is repeated from RLSS to DD-I (Regional) and vice versa then 30 seconds banking per episode can be utilised from RLSS to DD-I in the same programme within one month of telecast on RLSS.

Note: The procedures for the approval of the credit lines is the same as that for advertisements.

IV. REPEAT PROGRAMMES

Approval of a programme for a particular Channel does not mean that the programme is automatically approved for another Channel of Doordarshan. The programme has to be submitted fresh to a Channel for approval as per the extant policy. For a programme being repeated on a particular Channel, the telecast fee charged shall be according to the following schedule:

a) If a programme is repeated on the same Channel then 50% premium shall be charged on the telecast fee of the new slot.

b) If the programme is repeated from DD-2 to DD-1 then 50% premium will be charged on the telecast fee of the new slot on DD-1.

c) If a programme is repeated on DD-2 from DD-1 then 50% premium shall be charged on the telecast fee of the new slot.

d) If a programme is repeated on DD-2 from Regional Kendras, a premium of 25% shall be charged on the telecast fee of the new slot on DD-2.

e) If the programme is repeated on DD-2 from Regional Kendras, a premium of 25% will be added to Telecast / Sponsorship Fees of the slot on DD-2 with no change in FCT for the slot on DD-II.

f) If a programme is repeated on Regional Kendra / Hindi Belt from DD-1 / DD-2 then *a* premium of 25% shall be charged on the telecast fee of the new *slot.*

g) If a programme is repeated from one Regional Kendra / Hindi Belt to another Kendra / Hindi

Belt then 10% premium shall be charged on the telecast fee of the new slot.

h) If programme is repeated on any channel of Doordarshan from the DD-India then 10% premium shall be charged on the telecast fee of the new slot.

i) If any programme is repeated on DD-India from any other channel of Doordarshan then no premium shall be charged. Also, no premium will be charged if any programme is repeated from any channel of Doordarshan to the Regional Language Satellite Channel and vice versa as well as repeats within the Regional Language Satellite Channel.

V. BRANDING (for all programmes)

Full spot buy rate applicable for the said programme will be charged. This is applicable for the Regional Kendras also. For the branding purpose, the usage of the punchline for the product shall be allowed in the v/o for branding. For the purposes of branding, the producer / marketing agency shall be allowed not more than 5 seconds for the usage of the punchline of the product in the voice over for branding.

For branded quiz shows, interview based programmes and other programme where the microphone is visible in the camera frame, the producer can carry the brand of the product alongwith the name of the programme on the cube of the microphone.

VI. PRIZE SCHEME AND / OR CONTEST SCHEME

Prize Scheme / Contest scheme can be a part of FCT but if it goes beyond admissible FCT, the product/

agency will have to pay at the following flat rates:

Non-Prime Time Rs. 7,500/-
Prime Time Rs.10,000/-

If the Prize scheme / contest is not part of admissible FCT then it can go upto a maximum of one minute. In the prize scheme, the producer / marketing agency shall be allowed to announce and show the branded products being given as prizes.

VII. CANCELLATION CHARGES (for spots booking)

A contract can be canceled by an agency giving a notice of 7 days or more before the telecast date. If the notice is less than 7 days before the telecast date, billing will be done as per contract filed. However, if the marketing agency / producer are withdrawing from the agreement signed with the Sponsored Wing at the time of allotment of programme, then the mandatory notice as per the agreement shall apply.

VIII. ADVERTISEMENT DURATION

Advertisement of 5 seconds or in multiples of 5 seconds duration shall be accepted. Advertisement below 5 seconds will not be accepted. If the duration of the spot is above 5 seconds and below 10 seconds then it shall be charged for 10 seconds.

IX. TIME CHECK BEFORE NEWS

Mute advertisement for 5 to 10 seconds with either the name of the product or the client will be permitted. Logo product shot or product advertising is allowed / acceptable.

X (a) Doordarshan shall be entitled to review the category of a programme every quarter or after the telecast of 13 episodes. The review shall be based on the performance of the programme based on TRP ratings of the quarter.

(b) Same category and same telecast fee with the FCT applicable will continue till the end of that programme. For example, if a serial starts at 9.30 PM and continues till 11.30 PM, it will pay the same telecast fee per half an hour till 11.30 PM which is applicable at 9.30 PM. Doordarshan reserves the right to upgrade / downgrade the category of such telecasts on a case to case basis.

XI. All advertisements will be governed by the Code for Commercial Advertising for Doordarshan. Only advertisements approved by Doordarshan Commercial Service will be allowed for telecast. If any unapproved commercial is telecast, the agency will be black-listed and will also be charged penalty of five (5) times the rate of the normal spot buy for the programme where such advertisement appeared.

XII. All values in the Rate Card are in gross.

XIII. Spot buy rate unit = 10 seconds

Sponsorship Fee rate unit = 30 minutes

All programmes accepted for telecast on Doordarshan shall normally be of half an hour duration. However, programmes falling under the Public Service Broadcasting category, News and Current Affairs and Children's category can be of lesser or odd duration. In this case, all such programmes of 5 minutes, 10 minutes and odd durations etc. shall be charged on pro-rata basis rounded off to the nearest unit of 5 minutes. The FCT available shall also be on pro-rata basis of the relevant slot.

XIV. Programmes categorised under Public Service Broadcasting, News & Current Affairs and Children's category shall have concessional rates in non-prime time bands. However, no concession shall be available to these categories of programmes in the prime time / mid-prime time. In non-prime time, these programmes shall be charged at 75% of the slot fees and shall be allowed the admissible FCT of that slot.

XV. For the programme 'On Making of the Film", telecast fee will be four times the normal fee of the slot on DD-I and three times the prevalent telecast fee on DD-II.

XVI. For Teleshopping, the telecast fee shall be six times of the prevalent slot fee in which programme is telecast -both on DD-I and DD-II. This shall apply to regional channels also.

XVII. For the purpose of application of commercial terms in case of such programmes / serials which are telecast more than once in a week, all the episodes telecast in one particular week will be counted as one episode. For example, in case of such serials which are telecast five times a week, 130 episodes will be counted as 26 episodes for the purpose of application of commercial terms and 260 episodes for 52 weeks.

XVIII. i) Doordarshan is doing away with the charging of telecast fee for programme promo / branded promo and will henceforth allow branded promos / tag-on promos. As outlined in the sponsorship guidelines, henceforth, Doordarshan would take a one minute mid break in a programme for telecast of promos/special messages/ advertisements. The scheduling of the promos would be done by Doordarshan and requests/ contracts for telecast of promos would not be accepted anymore.

ii) The duration of the promo shall be 20 seconds which can include upto a maximum of 5 seconds for branding purposes.

XIX. Programmes rating low on the TAM would be immediately removed or shifted from the prime time. A programme shall be allotted only for 26 episodes and only such programmes which have good TRP in that slot would be given extension. According to the TAM data, TRPs of a programme become available within two weeks of a telecast of a programme and that will be monitored. If by the 13th week the programme is not able to establish itself, it is clear that it is not doing well in the market and the Sponsor Wing would remove the same and slot a new serial in its place.

XX. Each time band of Doordarshan will have a basic benchmark for TRP ratings, which will be utilised for monitoring the TRPs and continuance of slotted programmes. The TRP of all TV homes and SEC ABC 15+ females will be monitored for this purpose. According to the analysis, benchmark for the different time slots on DD-I will be as follows :

Prime Time : ratings between 6 and above.

Mid Prime Time: between 3-6

Time slot generating ratings below 3.

Early morning till 11.00 AM and late night slots after 11.00 PM.

XXI. In so far as categorisation in terms of film based and non-film based programmes for various channels are concerned, such categorisation will be made and decided by the Evaluation Committee depending on the film content of the programme and the telecast fee / rates will accordingly be made applicable.

XXII. Depending on commercial exigencies, Doordarshan can revise the commercial terms of a programme including but not limited to upgrading or downgrading the category of a programme or suitably revising the FCT and SBR both in cases of outside produced programme and DD produced / acquired programme.

XXIII. In case of any dispute or interpretation arising out of the Rate Card, the decision of Doordarshan will be final.

XXIV. The rates indicated in the Rate Card are the minimum that is to be charged for each slot. If more than two serials are available for a particular slot, the producer who agrees to pay higher telecast fee shall be allotted the slot with the admissible FCT remaining fixed.

CATEGORISATION

National Network (DD-1)

Prime Time

(i) 8.00 PM to 11.00 PM (Monday to Sunday).

(ii) 9.00 AM to 1.00 PM (Sunday).

Mid Prime Time

(i) 12.00 Noon to 2.00 PM (Monday to Friday)

Non-Prime Time

(i) 6.00 AM to 9.00 AM (Sunday).

(ii) 6.00 AM to 12.00 Noon except Sunday morning 9.00 AM to 1.00 PM

(iii) 6.00 AM to 7.00 PM (Saturday).

(iv) 1.00 PM to 4.00 PM (Sunday).

(v) 7.00 PM to 8.00 PM.

(vi) 11.00 PM onwards till 12.30 AM

Note : 1. In case of Doordarshan produced programmes, Telecast Fee / FCT will be as per time category prevailing there, but Doordarshan reserves the rights to increase the FCT subject to a maximum of total FCT time of 25% of the duration of the programme.

2. Chitrahaar and Rangoli are dealt separately with separate spot buy rate.

3. In so far as categorisation of film based and non-film based programmes for various channels is concerned, such categorisation will be decided by the Evaluation Committee depending on the film content of the programme and the telecast fee / rates will be 20% more than the telecast fee of the relevant slot.

NATIONAL NETWORK NEWS (SBR PER 10 SECONDS)

Before News / Mid Break

Samachar / News (8.00 PM / 8.30 PM)

75,000/- 85,000/-

Samachar / News (7.00 AM / 8.00 AM)

20,000/-

Samachar / News (2.00 PM / 2.10 PM)

20,000/-

Mukhya Samachar / Headlines

15,000/-

Time Check (8.00 PM / 8.30 PM)

35,000/-

Time Check

(Morning & Afternoon) 15,000/-

Note : 1. In Samachar and News (7.00 AM / 8.15 AM), there can be two breaks of 60 seconds each.

2. In Samachar and News (2.00 PM / 2.10 PM), there can be one break of 60 seconds or two breaks of 30 seconds each.

3. In Samachar and News (8.00 PM / 8.30 PM), there will be three breaks of 60 seconds each.

DD-I RATE CARD

Category SBR (in Rs.)

Sponsorship Fee (in Rs.)

FCT (in secs.)

I. Outside Produced

a) Prime Time

i) 9.00 PM -11.00 PM

(All days) 60,000/- 3,50,000/- 120

ii) 9.00 AM -1.00 PM

(Sunday) 60,000/- 3,50,000/- 120

b) Mid Prime Time

i) Afternoon Soaps

12.00 Noon 2.00 PM 15,000/- 1,50,000/- 150

c)	Non-Prime Time 15,000/- 50,000/-	150

Part-II

In-House / Doordarshan Produced / Commissioned / Royalty Programmes

a)	Prime Time 60,000/- 3, 50,000/-	120
b)	Mid-Prime Time 15,000/- 1, 50,000/-	150
c)	Non-Prime Time 15,000/- 50,000/-	150

Note : 1. Doordarshan, however, reserves the right to increase or decrease the FCT from programme to programme.

2. Dcordarshan can upgrade / downgrade the category of Doordarshan produced programmes as per requirements.

3. There shall be no hike after 26 episodes and thereafter for daily serials in the 11.00 AM -12.00 Noon band as this band gets curtailed by Parliament Question Hour.

4. For prime time, mid prime time and non prime time serials, there shall be a 25% hike after 26 episodes (irrespective of the number of episodes allotted) on the initial telecast fee of the slot. There shall be another l5% hike on the initial telecast fee after every 13th episode. In all cases the hike shall be calculated on the initial / original telecast fee of the slot.

5. The producer shall be allowed to buy extra additional commercial time upto 180 seconds in each half hour at SBR.

CATEGORISATION

Metro Entertainment Channel (DD-2)

Prime Time (i) 8.00 PM -10.30 PM (All days)

Mid Prime Time (i) 10.30 PM -11.00 PM

(ii) 1.00 PM -8.00 PM

(iii) 9.00 AM -1.00 PM (Sunday morning)

Non Prime Time (i) Rest of the time

DD-II RATE CARD

Category SBR	(in Rs.)
Sponsorship Fee	(in Rs.)
FCT	(in secs.)

I. Outside Produced

a) Prime Time

40,000/- 2,00,000/- 120

i) 8.00 PM -10.30 PM (All days)

b) Mid Prime Time 20,000/- 50,000/- 210

i) 10.30 PM -11.00 PM

ii) 7.00 PM -8.00 PM

iii) 9.00 AM -1.00 PM (Sunday morning)

c) Non Prime Time Rest of the time

10,000/- 15,000/- 210

II. Doordarshan Produced / Commissioned / Acquired Programmes

a) Prime Time 40,000/- 2,00,000/- 120

b) Mid Prime Time 20,000/- 50,000/- 210

c) Non-Prime Time 10,000/- 15,000/- 210

III. Urdu News 10,000/-

Note : 1. Doordarshan, however, reserves the right to increase or decrease the FCT from programme to programme.

2. Doordarshan can upgrade / downgrade the category of Doordarshan produced programmes as per the requirements.

3. The producer shall be allowed to buy extra additional commercial time upto 120 seconds in each half hour at SBR.

RATE CARD FOR DD NEWS CHANNEL

I.	Prime Time	-	7.30 PM -10.00 PM daily
II.	Non Prime Time	-	Remaining time zones other than Business Day for which separate Rate Card shall apply.

OUTSIDE PRODUCED / IN-HOUSE

Category SBR (in Rs.)

Sponsorship Fee (in Rs.)

FCT (in secs.)

Prime Time

2,000/- 5,000/- 210

Non-Prime Time

1,000/- 3,000/- 210

RATE CARD FOR BUSINESS DAY

S. No. Category Rate Remarks

1. ROS Spot Rs.1,000/- per 10 sees. ROS No positions guaranteed.
2. Fixed Spot Rs.2,000/- per 10 secs. at specified positions.
3. Co-Sponsorship Rs.20,000/- for half an hour with 150 secs. FCT 100 secs, to be utilised within the programme, the rest 50 secs, can be used as ROS on same day within Business Day programme.
4. Branded Sponsorship Rs.30,000/- for half hour with 150 secs. FCT 100 secs, to be utilised within the programme, the rest 50 secs, can be used as ROS on same day within Business Day programme.
5. Ticker Branding Rs.3 lacs for 1 month The brand logo would be displayed in the ticker, twice in the alphabet series A-Z depicting the price movements.
6. Graphic Sides Rs. 2 lacs for 1 month Right bottom corner for the brand name / logo.

Rs. 5 to Rs.10.01 lacs spend in 1 month.

The client will get 20% extra FCT on ROS basis.

Above Rs.10 lacs spend in 1 month. The client will get 35% extra FCT on ROS basis.

Note : The spends on ticker and graphics do not get entitled for any bonus spots.

R.O.S.

I. For advertisers willing to enter into an annual contract with Doordarshan and committing a revenue of Rs.1 Crore or more, we would offer the following package for the News Channel :-

a) 6000 exposures / spots of 10 seconds each on the News Channel on R.O.S. basis. These exposures (spots) will not be before News Bulletins or after News Bulletins and will also not be in-between two News Bulletins.

b) 100 exposures of 10 seconds each during the Evening News Bulletins at mid-break on DD-I.

II. For advertisers committing Rs.50 lacs on News Channel on ROS basis

a) 3000 exposures / spots of 10 seconds each on the News Channel.

b) 50 exposures / spots of 10 seconds each in the evening News Bulletins at mid-break on DD-I.

III. For advertisers committing Rs.25 lacs per year on News Channel

a) 1500 exposures / spots on the News Channel.

b) 25 exposures / spots of 10 seconds each in the evening News Bulletins at mid-break on DD-I.

Special package: Every one spot booked on DD-I prime time News (mid-break) in the evening and get 1 : 9 bonus at non-prime time on DD-News Channel on ROS basis.

DD SPORTS

	Outside Produced In-house	Production
Prime Events :-International cricket, tennis, football		
Sponsorship Fee (Rs.)	5,000/-	7,000/-
FCT (in secs.)	240	120
SBR per 10 secs. (Rs.)	2,000/-	2,000/-

Non-Prime Events:- Magazine programmes, Sports

News and other sports events

Sponsorship Fee (Rs.)	3,000/-	5,000/-
FCT (in secs.)	180	120
SBR per 10 secs. (Rs.)	1,000/-	2,000/-

ROS Package at other than prime time :

I. Rs.10 lacs -1500 spots of 10 seconds on DD-Sports Channel

II. Rs.5 lacs -700 spots of 10 seconds on DD-Sports Channel

III. Rs.1 lac -120 spots of 10 seconds on DD-Sports Channel

Note :

1. This ROS package shall not apply to cricketing events, football, hockey, tennis.
2. ROS package does not guarantee a spot at a fixed place.

DD INDIA

Telecast Fee per half an hour (in Rs.)

FCT (in secs.)

SBR per 10 secs.

A. Sponsored Programme

5,000/- 150 2,000/-

B. DD Produced Programme

5,000/- 150 2,000/-

C. Repeat Programme from DD-I / DD-II

(Existing programmes being telecast on DD-I / DD-II with a repeat on DD-India within a week.)

Nil

Nil 2,000/-

D. Repeat programmes other than covered in 'C' above.

Rs.1,000/- 60 2,000/-

ROS Package at other than prime time :

I. Rs.10 lacs -1500 spots of 10 seconds on DD-India Channel

II. Rs.5 lacs -700 spots of 10 seconds on DD-India Channel

III. Rs.1 lac -120 spots of 10 seconds on DD-India Channel

Note :

1. ROS package does not guarantee a spot at a fixed place.
2. The 30 seconds banking earlier available on DD-I is being discontinued.

DELHI LPT

Category SBR (in Rs.)

Sponsorship Fee (in Rs.)

FCT (in secs.)

I. Prime Time

i) 8.30 AM -9.00 AM (Sunday) (against News)

20,000/-

ii) After 7.00 PM & 7.30 PM 'except Wed., Sat. & Sun.)

15,000/- 25,000/- 150

II. Non-Prime Time

10,000/- 15,000/- 120

i) 4.00 PM to 7.00 PM

DOORDARSHAN IN-HOUSE PROGRAMMES

Category SBR (in Rs.)

Sponsorship Fee (in Rs.)

FCT (in secs.)

I. Prime Time

(i) 7.30 PM -8.00 PM 20,000/- Nil

(ii) 7.00 PM -7.30 PM (News)

(iii) 15,000/- 25,000/- 150

II. Non-Prime Time

10,000/- 15,000/- 120

Note : 1. Doordarshan reserves the right to increase or decrease the FCT from programme to programme.

DELHI HINDI BELT

2.30 PM -4.30 PM

OUTSIDE SPONSORED/IN-HOUSE PROGRAMMES

SBR (in Rs.)	15,000/-
Sponsorship Fee (in Rs.)	40,000/-
FCT (in secs.)	180

RATES AND ADMISSIBLE FCT FOR DOORDARSHAN PRODUCED / COMMISSIONED / ACQUIRED PROGRAMMES ON METRO NETWORK (DD—II)

Category SBR (in Rs.)

Sponsorship Fee (in Rs.)

FCT (in secs.)

a) Prime Time

i) (8.00 PM -10.30 PM) 25,000/- 1,40,000/- 150

b) Mid Prime Time

i) 10.30 PM -11.00 PM 15,000/- 35,000/- 150

ii) (9.00 AM -12.00 Noon)
(Sunday)

15,000/- 35,000/- 150

iii) 7.00 PM -8.00 PM

15,000/- 35,000/- 150

c) Non-Prime Time

10,000/- 15,000/- 150

RATES AND ADMISSIBLE FCT FOR SINGLE METRO OUTSIDE PRODUCED

FILM BASED (Delhi & Calcutta)

Telecast Fee Per half an hour (in Rs.)	15,000/-
FCT Per half an hour (in secs.)	150
Spot Buy Rate Per 10 secs. (in Rs.)	5,000/-

CHENNAI

Telecast Fee Per half an hour (in Rs.)	15,000/-
FCT Per half an hour (in secs.)	150
Spot Buy Rate Per 10 secs. (in Rs.)	6,000/-

NON-FILM BASED (Delhi, Calcutta & Chennai)

Story based / fiction based

Telecast Fee

Per half an hour (in Rs.) 10,000/-

FCT

Per half an hour (in secs.) 210

Spot Buy Rate

Per 10 secs. (in Rs.) 5,000/-

Delhi + Mumbai Service

Telecast Fee

Per half an hour (in Rs.) 15,000/-

FCT

Per half an hour (in sees.) 150

Spot Buy Rate

Per 10 secs. (in Rs.) 5,000/-

Film based	
Telecast Fee	
Per half an hour (in Rs.)	15,000/-
FCT	
Per half an hour (in sees.)	150
Spot Buy Rate	
Per 10 secs. (in Rs.)	5,000/-
Non-Film based	
Telecast Fee	
Per half an hour (in Rs.)	12, 500/-
FCT	
Per half an hour (in sees.)	210
Spot Buy Rate	
Per 10 secs. (in Rs.)	5,000/-

For non-film based, non-fiction serial, we were charging 50% less of the telec-ast fee of non-film bases. Same formula could be applied again.

DOORDARSHAN PRODUCED / COMMISSIONED

ACQUIRED PROGRAMME -Delhi Calcutta & Mumbai

SBR (in Rs.)

Sponsorship Fee (in Rs.)

FCT (in secs.)

FILM BASED 5,000/- 15,000/- 150

NON-FILM BASED 5,000/- 10,000/- 210

Chennai

FILM BASED 5,000/- 15,000/- 90

NON-FILM BASED 5,000/- 15,000/- 150

For non-film based, non-fiction serial, we were charging 50% less of the telecast fee of non-film bases. Same formula could be applied again.

Appendix-2

Advertising Code:

Code for commercial advertising on Doordarshan. It in-corporates the indecent Representation of women Act and the consumer Act, both of which were passed by parliament in 1986.

General rules for conduct in advertising :

1. Advertising shall be so designed as to conform to the laws of the country and shall not offend the morality, decency and the religious susceptibilities of the people.

2. No advertisement shall be permitted which:

   i) derides any race, caste, colour, creed and nationality;

   ii) is against any of the directive principles, or any other provision in the Constitution of India;

   iii) tends to incite people to crime or glorifies violence or obscenity in any way;

   iv) adversely affects friendly relations with foreign countries;

v) exploits the National emblem or any part of the constitution or the person or personality of a national leader or state dignitary.

vi) relates to or promotes cigarettes and tobacco products, liquor, wines and other intoxicants;

vii) in its depiction of women violates the Constitutional guarantees given to all citizens such as equality of status & opportunity and dignity of the individual. Women must not be portrayed in derogatory light and in a manner that emphasizes passive, submissive qualities and encourages them to play a subordinate and secondary role in family and in society. The portrayal of the female form shall be aesthetic and within the well established norms of good taste and decency.

3. No advertisement shall in any way be presented as News.

4. Advertisements must not be directed towards any religious or political ends or have any relation to any industrial dispute.

5. Advertisements for services concerned with the following services shall not be accepted:

i) money lenders

ii) chit funds

iii) savings schemes and lotteries other than those conducted by the Central & State Government organisations, Nationalised or recognised banks and public sector undertakings;

iv) unlicenced employment services

v) betting tips & guide books relating to horse racing or other games of chance.

6. No advertisement shall make claims to the effect that the product advertised posesses any miraculous or supernatural property or quality which is difficult of being proved, e.g. cure for baldness, skin whitener.
7. Scientific or statistical excerpts from technical literature etc. may be used only with a proper sense of responsibility to the ordinary viewer.
8. Advertisers or their agents must be ready to furnish evidence to substantiate any claims or illustrations since the Director General of DD has the right to demand the same.
9. Advertisements shall not contain disparaging or derogatory references to another product or service.
10. Testimonials must be genuine and used in a manner not to mislead viewers.
11. No advertisement shall be accepted which violates AIR and TV Broadcast code which is reproduced below

    i) Criticism of friendly countries;

    ii) Attack on religions or communities;

    iii) Anything obscene or defamatory;

    iv) incitement to violence or anything against maintenance of law & order;

    v) Anything amounting to contempt of court;

    vi) Aspersions against the integrity of the President and the Judiciary;

    vii) Anything affecting the integrity of the Nation; and

    viii) criticism by name of any person.
12. Information given to consumers in relation to the

price quality & weight of products shall be accurate.

13. Any pretence in advertising copy must be avioded. The simulation of appearance or voice of a personality in connection with the advertisements for commercial products requires a permission from the personality to that effect.
14. Advertisements for a product or a service shall not be accepted if it suggests that if children do not buy it they shall be lacking in their duty or loyalty to any person. Also if it is suggested in the advertisement that the children shall be condemned, ridiculed if they do not buy the product. The advertisements shall also not create in the children an interest to do something which can prove to be dangerous to the children.
15. No advertisement shall try to take advantage of the superstition or ignorance of the public.
16. Advertisements should be truthful, avoid distorting facts and misleading the public by means of implications and commissions.
17. Testimonials of any kind from experts etc. other than Government recognised standardisation agencies shall not be permitted.
18. Imitations likely to mislead the viewers shall be avoided.
19. Advertisements shall not be obscene, vulgar and offensive in their theme or treatment. This also applies to such advertisements which advertise objectionable books or photographs.
20. For advertising for medicines the following guidelines have been laid down:

    i) No advertisement shall contain a claim to cure any ailment or symptoms of ill health.

ii) There should be no exaggerated claims regarding the composition, character, action and suitability of the purpose for which it is recommended.

iii) Appeals to fear shall not be made.

iv) Advertisements for diagnosis or treatment by correspondence are strictly prohibited.

v) When words such as college, clinic, institute, laboratory are used in advertisements, such references can be made only when the said establishment does actually exist.

vi) Advertisements for products specifically offered to women shall not be advertised as products that are effective in inducing miscarriage.

vii) Advertisements relating to claims about curing of sexual weakness, premature ageing, loss of virility, sexual excesses etc. shall not be accepted.

viii) No advertisements should offer any medical product that is for the purposes of slimming, weight reduction or figure control.

ix) No advertisement shall contain any offer to diagnose or treat complaints or conditions by hypnosis

Appendix-3

THE CABLE TELEVISION NETWORKS (REGULATION) AMENDMENT BILL, 2002

A BILL further to amend the Cable Television Networks (Regulation) Act, 1995

Be it enacted by Parliament in the Fifty-third Year of the Republic of India as follows:

1. This act may be called the Cable Television Networks (Regulation) Amendment Act 2002
2. In the Cable Television Networks (Regulation) Act, 1995 (hereinafter referred to as the principal Act) after section 4, the following section shall be inserted, namely: -

'4A. (1). Where the Central Government is satisfied that it is necessary in the public interest to do so, it may, by notification in the Official Gazzette, make it obligatory for every cable TV operator to transmit or retransmit programme of any pay channel through an addressable system with effect from such date as may be specified in the notification and different dates may be specified for different states, cities, towns or areas as the case may be.

(2) If the Central Government is satisfied that it is necessary in the public interest so to do, it may by notification in the Official Gazette, specify one or more free to air channels to be included in the package of channels forming the basic service tier and any or more such channels may be specified, in the notification genre wise for providing a programme mix of entertainment, information, and education, and such other programmes.

(3) The Central government may specify in the notification referred to in subsection (2), the number of free to air channels to be included in the package of channels forming basic service tier for the purpose of that sub-section and different numbers may be specified for different States, cities, towns or areas as the case may be.

(4) If the Central Government is satisfied that it is necessary in the public interest so to do it may by notification in the Official Gazette specify the maximum amount which a cable operator may demand from the subscriber for receiving the programmes transmitted in the basic service tier provided by such cable operator.

(5) Notwithstanding anything contained in the sub-section (4), the Central Government may, for the purposes of that sub-section, specify in a notification referred to in that sub-section different maximum amounts for different States, cities, towns or areas as the case may be.

(6) Notwithstanding anything contained in this section programmes of basic service tier shall be receivable by any subscriber on the receiver set of a type existing immediately before the commencement of the Cable Television Networks (Regulation) Amendment Act 2002 without any addressable system attached with such receiver set in any manner.

(7) Every cable operator shall publicise, in the prescribed manner, to the subscribers the subscription rates and the periodic intervals after which such subscriptions are payable for receiving each pay channel provided by such cable operator.

(8) The cable operator shall not require any subscriber to have a receiver set of a particular type to receive signals of cable television network.

Provided that the customer shall use an addressable system to be attached to his receiver set for receiving programmes transmitted on pay channel.

(9) Every cable operator shall submit a report to the Central Government in the prescribed form and manner containing the information regarding:-

...(i) the number of total subscribers: ....

...(ii) subscription rates:

...(iii) number of subscribers receiving programmes transmitted in basic service tier or particular programme or set of programmes transmitted on pay channel.

In respect of cable services provided by such cable operator through a cable television network and such report shall be submitted periodically at such intervals as may be prescribed and shall also contain the rate of amount, if any, payable by the cable operator to any broadcaster.

.... Explanation -For the purpose of this section:-

(a) "addressable system" means an electronic device or more than one electronic devices put in an integrated system through which signals of cable television network can be sent in encrypted or unencrypted form, which can be decoded by the device or devices at the premises of the subscriber within the limits of authorisation made, on the choice and request of such subscribers, by the cable operator to the subscriber. ....

(b) "basic service tier" means a package of free-to-air channels provided by a cable operator, for a single price to the subscribers of the area in which his cable television network is providing service and such channels are receivable for viewing by the subscribers on the receiver set of a type existing immediately before the commencement of the Cable Television Network (Regulation) Amendment Act, 2002 without any addressable system attached to such receiver set in any manner.

(c) "channel" means a set of frequencies used for transmission of a programme.

(d) "encrypted" in respect of a signal of cable television network means the changing of such signals in a systematic way so that the signal would be unintelligible without a suitable receiving equipment and the expression "unencrypted" shall be construed accordingly.

(e) "free-to-air channel", in respect of a cable

television network means that a channel, the reception of which would not require the use of an addressable system to be attached with the receiver set of the subscriber.

(f) "pay channel", in respect of a cable television network, means a channel the reception of which by the subscriber would require the use of an addressable system to be attached to his receiver set.

3. In section 9 of the principal Act, the following provision shall be inserted, namely:- "Provided that the equipment required for the purposes of section 4A shall be installed by the cable operator in his CATV network within six months from the date, specified in the notification issued under sub-section (1) of section 4A in accordance with the provisions of the said Act for the said purposes".

4. In section 11 of the principal Act in the sub-section (1), after the word and figure " section 3", the figure and letter" 4A", shall be inserted.

5. Section 16 of the principal Act shall be numbered as sub-section (1) thereof and after sub-section (1) as so numbered, the following sub-section shall be inserted namely:-

"(2) Notwithstanding anything contained in the Code of Criminal Procedure 1973, the contravention of section 4A shall be a cognisable offence under this section".

6. In section 25 of the principal Act in sub-section (2),... (i) after clause (a), the following clauses shall be inserted, namely:-"

(aa) the manner of publicising the subscription rates and the periodical intervals at which such subscriptions are payable under sub-section (7) of section 4A;

(aaa) the form and manner of submitting report under sub-section (9) of section 4A and the interval at which such report shall be submitted under that sub-section".

Appendix-4

Telecom Regulatory Authority of India
Notification

New Delhi January 15, 2004 / Pausa 25, 1925

No. 301-3/2004-Eco

In exercise of the powers conferred upon it under sub-section (2) of section 11 of the TRAI Act, 1997 as amended read with the Notification No.39 dated 09.01.2004 issued from file No. 13-1/2004-Restg. by the Government of India under clause (d) of sub-section (1) of section 11 and proviso to clause (k) of section 2 of the Telecom Regulatory Authority of India Act, 1997 to notify, by an Order in the Official Gazette, tariffs at which Telecommunications (Broadcasting and Cable Operation) Services shall be provided, the Telecom Regulatory Authority of India hereby makes the following Order.

THE TELECOMMUNICATION (BROADCASTING AND CABLE)

SERVICES TARIFF ORDER 2004
[1 of 2004]
Section-I
Title, Extent and Commencement

1. Short title, extent and commencement:

   i. This Order shall be called "The Telecommunication (Broadcasting and Cable) Services Tariff Order 2004".

   ii. The Order shall cover tariffs for all Telecommunication (Broadcasting and Cable) Services throughout the territory of India as also those originating in India or outside India and terminating in India.

   iii. The Order shall come into force on the date of its notification in the Official Gazette.

Section II. Tariff

2. The charges payable by

   (a) Cable subscribers to cable operator;

   (b) Cable operators to Multi Service Operators/ Broadcasters (including their authorised distribution agencies); and

   (c) Multi Service Operators to Broadcasters (including their authorised distribution agencies)

   prevalent as on 26th December 2003 shall be the ceiling with respect to both free-to-air and pay channels, both for CAS and non-CAS areas until final determination by Telecom Regulatory

Authority of India on the various issues concerning these charges.

Section III

3. Explanatory Memorandum

Annex A to this Order contains an Explanatory Memorandum for the issue of this Order.

Section IV

4. Interpretation

In case of dispute regarding interpretation of any of the provisions of this Order, the decision of the Authority shall be final and binding.

BY ORDER

Dr. Harsha Vardhana Singh

Principal Advisor cum Secretary
Telecom Regulatory Authority of India

Annexture

Explanatory Memorandum

Cable Television Networks (Regulation) Act, 1995 was amended in 2002 and Section 4A was inserted in the original Act which envisages "Transmission of programmes through addressable system" [popularly referred to as Conditional Access System (CAS)] with effect from such date as may be specified in the Notification. A Notification dated 14th January 2003 was issued by the Ministry of Information and Broadcasting, Government of India making it obligatory for every cable operator to transmit/re-transmit programmes of every pay channel through an addressable system in Chennai Metropolitan area, Municipal Council of Greater Mumbai area, Kolkata Metropolitan area and National Capital Territory of Delhi within six months from 15th day of January, 2003. Subsequently vide Notification dated 10th July, 2003 the date of implementation was deferred and fixed within six months from 1st March, 2003, and Chennai and the areas of NCT of Delhi, Kolkata, Mumbai to be covered by CAS were also specified. Thereafter vide

Notification dated 29th August, 2003, the earlier Notification dated 10th July, 2003 was amended and areas in NCT of Delhi where CAS was to be implemented were deleted.

2. The Hon'ble Delhi High Court, vide orders dated 4th December 2003, quashed the Notification dated 29th August 2003 issued by Ministry of Information & Broadcasting, Government of India. The cable operators of the notified areas partially withdrew pay channels from mid-night of 15th December 2003.

3. Delhi High Court in CW no. 8993-4/2003 in its order dated 26.12.03 allowed the implementation of CAS in Delhi. The Delhi High Court further directed that after expiry of three months, appropriate direction shall be issued after taking into consideration the feed back of three months' experience.

3. The Government of India issued a Notification No. 39 dated 9th January 2004 whereby, under the proviso to clause (k) of sub-section (1) of section 2 of the TRAI Act, 1997 as amended, the scope of the expression telecommunication services was increased to include the broadcasting services and cable services also. Thus, the broadcasting and cable services also came within the purview of the Telecom Regulatory Authority of India. Through this Notification, in exercise of the powers under clause (d) of sub-section (1) of section 11, the Telecom Regulatory Authority of India was further authorised to, inter-alia, specify standard norms for and periodicity of revision of rates of pay channels including interim measures.

4. There is considerable uncertainty about different aspects of the Conditional Access System (CAS) regime and a detailed examination is required of the various

issues, including the rates for the broadcast and cable services in CAS and non-CAS areas. Not only are there no standard rates or conditions at which services are provided by the cable operators to the subscribers, there are reports that there may be an increase in the rates charged to the subscribers. The Authority has begun its process of examination of the relevant issues, including those relating to CAS, through a consultation process. To bring some certainty in the rates prevailing for these services, it was considered necessary by the Telecom Regulatory Authority of India to intervene in the matter. The TRAI has, therefore, deemed it appropriate to specify as ceiling the rates at which the charges will be paid by the cable subscribers to cable operators, by the cable operators to multi service operators and by multi service operators to broadcasters, as those prevailing on 26th December 2003 with respect to both free-to-air channels and pay channels, and for both CAS and non-CAS areas. This intervention will continue until a final determination by the Telecom Regulatory Authority of India on the various issues involved. The Hon'ble Delhi High Court, in CW No. 8993-4/2003 dated 26th December 2003, directed the continuance of implementation of CAS in Delhi on a trial basis, initially for a period of three months, after which appropriate directions would be issued after taking into account the feedback for the three months' experience. The ceiling rates have therefore been specified as those prevailing on 26th December, 2003.

Bibliography

- Appadurai, A.(1996), Modernity at Large: Cultural Dimensions of Globalization, University of Minnesto Press, Minneaspolis.
- ---------- (ed.) (1986), The Social Life of Things: Commodities in Cultural Perspective, Cambridge University Press, Cambridge.
- Aggrawal, B.C. (1997), The Meaning of Hinglish-ness: Liberalization and Globalization in Indian Broadcasting, in programming for people from Cultural Rights to Cultural Responsibilities, (ed.) Kevin Robins, United Nations World Television Forum.
- Artz, Lee(2005), Paradigm Shudder in Global Media Journal, Vol-4, Issue-6, Purdue University, Calumet
- Baker, Chris(1997), Global Television: An Introduction, Blackwell Publishing.

- -----------(1999), Television Globalization and Cultural Identities, Open University Press, Buckingham, London.
- Boyd-Barret, O & Newbold, C (ed.)(1995), Approaches to Media: A Reader, Tunbridge Wells, Grey Publishing
- -----------(1998), Media Imperialism, Reformulated in Electronic Empires: Global Media and Local Resistance, Arnold, London.
- Bajpai, S & Unnikrishnan, N(1996) The Impact of Television Advertising on Children, Sage Publication, Delhi/London
- Banerjee, I (2002), Media Globalization and Localization in the New Asian TV Landscape, The International Journal for Communication Studies.
- Bicket, Douglas (2005), Reconsidering Geocultural Contraflow, Global Media Journal, Vol-4, Issue-6
- Bhatt, SC. Satellite Invasion of India, Gyan Publishing House, New Delhi.
- Chaterjee, PC (1991), Broadcasting in India, Sage, London.
- Crane, Diana. Cultural Globalization from the Perspective of the Sociology of Culture, University of Pennsylvania, USA.
- Chomsky, Noam (1989), Necessary Illusions: Thought Control in Democratic Societies, South End Press, Boston.
- Cichetto, Lynne(2004), Advertising and Globalization in India, Massey University, Wellington, Newzealand.
- Dass Biswajit (1997), Mass Media: Report of 50 Years of Communication Growth in India; Mimographed.

- Durham, M. G. Kellner, DM (eds.) (2001), Media and Cultural Studies: Key Works, Blackwell Publishers: Malden.
- Eashwar, S. Sucharita (ed.)(2003), Response to Globalization and the Digital Divide in the Asia-Pacific, Asia-Pacific Institute of Broadcasting, Singapore.
- Ferguson, M. (1995), Media Market and Identities: Reflections on the Global-Local Dialectic, University of Maryland, USA, in Canadian Journal of Media.
- Flavins, Stan (2003), On the Future of Global Television: An Economic and Historical Approach to Understanding the Basics and Trajectory of World Television in The Ad Astra, 2(1)2003, Young Romanian Scientists Journal International Peace Academy, New York.
- Gupta, Nilanjana (1998), Switching Channels: Ideologies of Television in India, Oxford University Press, New Delhi
- Griffin, M. (2002), Cultural Imperialism to Trans-national Commercialization, Global Media Journal, Vol-l.
- Goonesekera, Anura (1993), Media Technology and Social Imperatives: An Examination of Commu-nication Policies in Selected Asian Countries, Media Asia, Vol-20, No-4, AMIC, Singapore.
- ---------- Global Satellite Broadcasting Service: Educational and Cultural Contribution in Cultural and Educational Dimensions, UNESCO, Paris, C-11, 96/WS/8.
- Harris, Grey (1984), The Globalization of Adverti-sing in International Journal of Advertising, Vol-3.

- Herman, E and Robert, Mcchesney (1997), The Global Media : The New Missionaries of Global Capitalism, London.
- Handbook on Public Service Broadcasting, UNESCO, Paris.
- Indian Entertainment Industry Focus: 2010, Dreams to Reality-A CII-KPMG Report(pg.23-44).
- Joshi, SR & Trivedi, Bela (1994), Mass Media and Cross-Cultural Communication: A Study of Television in India, Development and Communication Unit, ISRO, Ahmedabad.
- Joshi, SR (1998), Transponder Television in India, in Goonesekera, A & Lee, P(eds.) TV Without Borders, Asia Speaks Out, AMIC, Singapore.
- Jagopal, A. (1993), The Rise of National Programming: The Case of Indian Television, Media Culture and Society, London.
- J. Bergland, A.Furnham & Barrie, Gunter (2002), Memory for Television Advertisement as a Function of Advertisement Programme Congruity in Applied Cogonitive Psychology, John Wileya Sons Ltd.
- Khushu, OP (1993), Satellite Communication in Asia: An Overview, Media Asia, Singapore.
- Kumar, Aashish (1999), Localizing The Global India: New Imperative for International Communication Scholarship in the Satellite Era, TBS, Adham Centre for TV Journalism, American University, Cairo.
- Kasser, T (2002), The High Price of Materialism, Brandford Books/MIT Press, Cambridge.
- Kumar, Kewal J (1981), Mass Communication in India, Jaico Publications, Delhi.

- McMillian, Divya. C (2003), Television, Gender and Labour in the Global City, Journal of Communication, (53)3, (496-511)
- McMillian, Divya. C (1999), Identity and Consumerism on Television in India, University of Washington, Tacoma.
- Mac Bride, Sean (1980), Many Voices One World, UNESCO, Paris.
- McLuhan.M. Understanding Media: In McQuail, D (1994), Mass Communication Theory, Sage, London.
- Melkote, Srinivas, R.P. Shields and Aggarwal, B.C. (eds.) (1998), International Broadcasting in Asia: Political and Cultural Implications, University Press of America, Lanham, Md.
- Melkote Srinivas R., Peter Shields Binod C. Agrawal eds. (1998), International Broadcasting in Asia: Political and Cultural Implications University Press of America, Lanham, Md.
- Modoux, Alain(ed.) (1997), World Communication Report: The Media and the Challenge of New Technologies, Chapter on Media Globalization and Regulation, UNESCO, Paris.
- Mukherjee, Arpita (2004), Trade and Culture(draft paper), UNESCO.
- Ninan, Sevanti (1995), Through the Magic Window: Television and Change in India, Sage, Delhi.
- O'Guinn Thomas C & LJ, Shrum (1997), The Role of Television in the Construction of Consumer Reality, Journal of Consumer Research (23)4, (278-294).
- Pathania, Geetika. Responses To Transnational TV in a STAR StuckLand: DD & STAR TV in India in

Melkote, SR Sheilds & Agrawal, BC(eds.) International Satellite Broadcasting in Asia, University Press of America, Marlyland.

- Postill, John (2005), Media Anthropology in a World of States(draft report), Bik, University of Bremen.
- Robert, Goldman (1992), Reading Ads Socially, Routledge, London.
- Robert, McChesney (2001), Global Media, Neo-liberalism and Imperialism, Monthly Review, Vol-52, No-10.
- Rothschild, Emma (1999), Globalization and the Return of History, Foreign Policy, Summer.
- Slater, Don (1992), Consumer, Culture & Modernity, Polity Press, Cambridge.
- Sepstrup, P & Goonesekera, A. (1994), TV Trans-nationalization: Europe and Asia, UNESCO, Paris.
- Straubhaar, J (2003), Choosing National Television: Cultural, Capital, Language and Cultural Proximity in Brazil in Elasmer, M(ed.) The Impact of International Television: A Paradigm Shift, LEA Publishers, London.
- Sinclair, John & Mark Harrison, Globalization and Television in India and China, Victoria University of Technology, Australia.
- Schiller, HI (1988), Current Views of Information and Media Power in Christian Academy(ed.)in The World Community in Post-Industrial Society, Seoul Wooseok Publishing Co.
- Sinha, SK (2004), Sociology of Media: Impact of Doordarshan on Tribals, Raj Publications, New Delhi.
- Srikandath , S. (1991), Cultural Values Depiction

in Indian Television Advertising, International Journal Of Mass Communication Studies.

- Suresh, N. (1996), Sustainable Consumption in Consumer Unity and Trust Society Magazine,3-B, Camac Street, Calcutta.
- Scott, Margaret (1991), News From No Where in Far Eastern Economic Review.
- Tomlinson, J (1991), Cultural Imperialism, John Hopkins University Press, Baltimore.
- Tomlinson, J (1997), Cultural Globalization and Cultural Imperialism., International Communication and Globalization: A Critical Introduction. (Ed.) Ali Mohammadi, Sage, London.
- -----------(1996), Globalization and Culture. The University of Chicago Press, Chicago.
- Thussu, DK, Indian Media: From Colonial to Global (ed.) University of North London.
- -----------, Introduction in Electronic Empires; Global Media and Local Resistance, Arnold, London.
- -----------(1998), Localizing the Global ZEE in India. Television Asia-December, 2003.
- TRAI Recommendation on Issues Relating To Broadcasting and Distribution of TV Channels (2004) Chapter on Advertising, Government of India, New Delhi.
- United States Department of Commerce, National Telecommunication and Information Administration, (1993) Globalization of Mass Media, General Printing Office, Washington.
- (Dr.) Ulla Carlsson. The Rise and Fall of NWICO and Then, NORDICOM, Goteborg University, Box-713, SE405 30, Goteborg.

- Vilanilam, J (1989), Television Advertising and the Indian Poor, in Media, Culture and Society, London.
- Werner, Vom. Busch (ed.)(2004), The Asian Media Directory, Konard-Adenauer Foundation, Singapore.
- Waters, M. (1995), Globalization, Routledge, London.
- Yogendra Singh (2000) Cultural Change in India, Rawat Publications, Jaipur.

Periodicals/Papers/Articles/Reports

- Rao, S. (1996), The Selling of Global Cultural Difference, in Sanskriti, Vol-7, Issue-2, No-1.
- Sehgal, R. (2000), Sunny Skies Ahead For Indian Channels.
- Thussu, DK., Taming The Dragon And The Elephant : Murdoch's Media in Asia.
- Ahmed, N., Cross Cultural Content Analysia of Advertising From US and India.
- Jena, SK (2000), Globalization and Popular Culture: Reading Advertisement Sociologically (seminar paper in collaboration with JNU & Albert Ludwigs University, Freibing)
- Rai, Vivek. Media Studies Conference 2002-Media and Globalization.
- Desai, Mira Kapil. Monographic: Indian Television in the Era of Globalization; Unity, Diversity or Disparity ?, SNDT Women University, Bombay.
- Dixit, Kunda . Star Wars : Conflicts and Media in the Satellite Age.

- Rohit & Vikas RM. Media: Rising Consumer Culture and the Working Class, IIT, Kanpur
- Pathania, Geetika. When Global Companies Localize: Adaptive Strategies of Media Companies Entering India., Austin University of Texas (Ph.D Dissertation, 1998)
- Blakley, Johanna. Entertainment Goes Global: Mass Culture in Transforming World, Norman Lear Centre & Pacific Council of International Policy.
- Krivocheev. World Vision-2000: A Proposed World Wide Forum on the Emerging Television Enviornment, EBV Technical Review, Summer, 1996.
- Indian Television Dot com's Ad-Wise-2002.
- Satellite and Cable TV-1999 & 2003 Publication.
- Broadcasting in India : Broadcasting Sector, July-1999 Review.
- UTV Software Communication Ltd; Draft Red Herring Prospectus-2004.
- Management Discussion and Analysis-ZEE Telefilms Ltd; Report.
- TV Today Network Prospectus, December-2003 and 2004 Report.
- The Tribune, July' 2005.
- Nimbus Television Pvt; Ltd;, Annual Report-2004.
- McKinsey Quarterly Report: Media and Entertainment, Various Issues.
- Rai University (lesson-19) Ethics in Advertising : ASCI Code for Commercial Advertising on Doordarshan in Indian Advertising.

- Rai University (lesson-7) Power of Television in Development.
- Advertising: World Federation of Advertisers-2000, EACA & UNEP.
- Tej, Bhatia (2000), Advertising in Rural India: Language, Marketing, Communication and Consumerism, Institute for the Study of Language and Culture of Asia & Africa, Tokyo Press, Tokyo, Japan.
- Business World Marketing White Book-2003-04.
- Basu, Aparimita. Media Laws: An Overview (thesis)
- FICCI-Arthur Andersen India Pvt; Ltd; Report - Indian Entertainment Industry: Envisioning for Tomorrow, March' 2001.
- -----do---- Strategy and Vision, March' 2000.
- The Economic Times, Entertainment 2001-02 issue.
- Directory of Indian Television Industry-1996 issue.
- Daniel, A Pope(1983) The Making of Modern Advertising (article)
- Economist: Sticky Issue-24 August'2002.
- Joshi, Subhash. 25 Years of Satellite Broadcasting in India.
- Bloomberg Television (2002) Pay TV in the Year 2002: Time for a Reality Check.
- The Hindu, 17 June' 2001-Television Software: Future Content.
- TRAI various notifications related to Cable & Satellite Channels in India, Govt. of India, New Delhi.
- Igal, Brightman. Television Networks in the 21st

Century: Growing Critical Mass in a Fragmenting World, Deloitte.

- Prof. Pisters Patricia, Transnationalism and Multiculturalism, ASCA.
- Gambaro, Marco (2003), The Evolution of Public Service Television: Methods of Financing and Implications For the Consumer.
- Cultural Work and Cultural Production: An Attempt to Survey a Seemingly Unending Field, Leonar Camauer-2002, Arbetslivsinstituteh.
- Paper on Globalization and Localization from an extended paper on Globalization and Satellite Television: New Technology and Cultural Dominance, Conference-Beijing Broadcasting Institute, Beijing, April 14-15, 2002.
- Rainer, Welzel. Asian Media in the Change and the Global Media Market.
- Khan, Habibul Haque (2004) Glocaliztıon as Globalization: Evoulation of a Sociological Concept, Journal of Sociology, Vol-1, No-2, Bangladesh.
- Goonesekera, A. Freedom in the Age of Global Communication.
- Hindustan Times, Control Regime for News Channels, 6 December' 2005.
- Hindustan Times, Panel to Develop Media, Entertainment Sectors. 28 December' 2005.
- The Hindu, Hasan Suroor 'Indian TV Channels invade Britain', 9 January' 2006.
- Hindustan Times Editorial: "Dourdarshan" 12 January, 2006.
- Bella, Thomas Worldpress.Org-Media: Satellite Television (prospect' 2003), London.

Reports/Papers on Doordarshan/Ministry of I & B/Government of India:

- Annual Report-2000-01, 02 & 2004-05, Ministry of Information & Broadcasting, Government of India, New Delhi.
- Doordarshan India-2003, Prasar Bharti (BCI), Directorate General, Doordarshan, New Delhi.
- Report of the Review Committee on the Working of Prasar Bharti, Ministry of Information & Broadcasting, Government of India. New Delhi.
- An Indian Personality For Television-Report of the Working Group on Software for Doordarshan, Vol-1 & 2, Publication Division, Ministry of I & B, Govt. of India, New Delhi.
- India-1998, Ministry of I & B, Publication Division, Govt. of India, New Delhi.
- Prasar Bharti Act-1990 (1996), Ministry of I & B, Govt. of India, New Delhi.
- Report on Prasar Bharti (Nitish Sen Gupta Committee-1996), Government of India, New Delhi.
- Cable Television Networks (Regulation) Act-2002 & 05, TRAI, New Delhi.
- Report of the Steering Committee on Communication and Information, (Tenth five year plan: 2002-07) Planning Commission, May' 2002, Government of India, New Delhi.
- Indian Television.Com.
- WWW.DDlndia.com

Index

❑ ❑ ❑